Ask the fish Keeper

MARC MORRONE
with Amy Fernandez

Original Illustrations © 2009 by Jason O'Malley. Photographs © 2009 by Gina Cioli/ Pamela Hunnicutt BowTie Studio, Clay Jackson, Anthony Terceira, Oliver Lucanus, Mark Smith, Alf Jacob Nilsen, Jay Hemdal, David Miller, Laurence Azoulay, and Shutterstock.com.

Library of Congress Cataloging-in-Publication Data

Morrone, Marc, 1960-
  [Ask the fish keeper]
  Marc Morrone's ask the fish keeper / by Marc Morrone with Amy Fernandez.
      p. cm.
  ISBN 978-1-933958-32-3
  1. Aquarium fishes—Miscellanea. 2. Aquarium fishes—Health—Miscellanea. I. Fernandez, Amy. II. Title. III. Title: Ask the fish keeper.
  SF457.M67 2009
  639.34—dc22
                          2009009829

BowTie Press®
A Division of BowTie, Inc.
3 Burroughs
Irvine, California 92618

Printed and bound in Singapore
16 15 14 13 12 11 10 09   1 2 3 4 5 6 7 8 9 10

To Dr. Herbert Axelrod,
my childhood hero in the fish world!

CONTENTS

For the Love of Tropical Fish

My longtime associate Andrew DePrisco phoned me and said, "Hey, Dr. A., I think I found your biggest fan. You're one of his heroes. His name is Marc Morrone. He's the pet expert from *The Martha Stewart Show*!"

My initial reaction, which will tell you a lot about my interest in television, was, "Martha who?" I regret that I had never heard of Marc Morrone, either. As it turns out, Marc Morrone and I have been living parallel lives, separated by several decades and, now, thousands of miles of ocean (in which the fish we both love swim day and night).

Both Marc and I shared a childhood fascination with tropical fish: I, in Bayonne, New Jersey, in the 1930s and Marc, about forty miles away in Long Island, New York, in the 1960s. Just before Marc was born, in the late 1950s, I discovered the cardinal tetra, *Paracheirodon axelrodi,* one of several popular fishes to bear my name. By the time five-year-old Marc had his first 10-gallon tank, in 1965, I had been publishing *Tropical Fish Hobbyist* magazine for over a dozen years as part of T.F.H. Publications, Inc., a company I had founded and that had become the world's largest publisher of pet books. Even today, I'm still proud that *Dr. Axelrod's Atlas of Freshwater Aquarium Fishes,* originally published in 1985 and now in its eleventh edition, remains one of the world's best-selling titles on tropical fishes. Of the hundred or so books I've written, it remains a personal favorite, too.

Marc still tells the story about how excited he was when his copy of *Tropical Fish Hobbyist* arrived each month. He's been a loyal reader since 1970, when he began following my fish-collecting expeditions in the waters of South America and Africa. To me, nothing else ever has been as exciting as hunting for—and occasionally discovering—new species of fishes, and I'm glad that I've been able to introduce others to the thrill of the chase.

I also discovered that Marc and I both love pet shops! Marc owned his first pet shop when he was just eighteen years old. I met my beautiful wife of fifty-three years, Evelyn, while she was working at her dad's pet shop (before Marc was a twinkle in his dad's eye!).

I'm delighted to be introducing you to Marc's first book on fish keeping. Marc, like me, is a self-taught fish doctor and keeper. Every answer Marc offers in this terrific little book comes from his years of experience working with fish in his home and in his shop. I'm highly gratified that the newer generations continue to love tropical fish as much as I have all these years!

—Dr. Herbert R. Axelrod
Zürich, Switzerland
March 2009

INTRODUCTION

Have you ever heard the saying "Give a man a fish, and he eats for a day; teach a man to fish, and he eats for the rest of his life"? That principle also applies to fish keeping. When I discussed this project with the editors of this book, there was a bit of controversy about what we should include. People who keep reef tanks may care little about saltwater fish tanks. People who keep saltwater tanks often have no interest in the freshwater discus fish, and people who keep the egg-laying discus may not want to read about live-bearing fish. In this hobby, everyone tends to focus on his or her own particular area of interest. However, no matter what type of aquatic pets people may have, everyone seems to have questions about what these animals need to stay healthy.

Fish keepers tend to ask the advice of other hobbyists or so-called experts and accept any answer that they get. This book is designed to encourage all aquarists to look at the residents of your aquarium from a different perspective. Many people think of the fish in their tanks as consumer products, computer chips, or CDs: you just pop a fish in the tank and watch. But fish are much more complicated than

that. They can see in color and have far greater cognitive powers than most people realize. Anyone who has attempted to catch a savvy largemouth bass can attest to this. Fish recognize each other as well as humans, and they can learn various behaviors through positive reinforcement training just as dogs and cats do.

The first step in finding answers to your questions about your fish is to take the time to observe them. As a child, I would sit in front of my 10-gallon tank, watching my fish for hours. I knew every fish as an individual. It's a pity that more modern-day aquarists don't devote as much time to this. Fish are still pets in our care, and any aquarium is comparable to a little zoo in your living room. You need to be aware of the quality of this environment and the denizens inhabiting it because they are totally dependent on you. If fish keepers spent more time studying their fish as animals and as individuals, they would have far fewer problems.

The next step, especially if you are having trouble with your kind of fish, is to learn something about its natural habitat and diet. Once you do, it becomes your job as a pet keeper to duplicate all of these factors as closely as possible. You must compare the animal's natural environment to the husbandry and habitat you have provided in the tank.

Fish are grouped according to family, genus, and species. For instance, majestic angels, blue-faced angels, and imperator angels are in one classification. Butterfly fish such as longnosed butterflies, copper band butterflies, and falcula butterflies are in another classification. The group of tangs includes yellow tangs and purple tangs. Many books provide detailed information on the biology, life histories, ecological niches, and so on of saltwater and freshwater fish. I really think it important that fish keepers study this type of information. If they understand their fish better, they can do much more to provide good habitats and help their fish to thrive. Unfortunately, you cannot not just depend on advice from someone who works in a fish store. Some fish store employees really don't know as much as they should. And there is no guarantee that a pretty fish you see in the pet store will be a suitable resident for your home aquarium. It is your responsibility as a fish keeper to go home and hit the books. Find out where a particular fish fits into the order of nature, so you will know where it fits—and whether it fits at all—into your home aquarium.

Feeding Picky Fish

There are many reasons why some fish don't eat in captivity. For instance, many fish are caught in ways, such as with drugs, that cause them to start dying as soon as they are removed from the water. Some wild-caught marine fish may take two months to slowly waste away. You can't put a fish on an IV. Other fish don't eat because they are not used to the foods they are offered in captivity. Today, pet shop freezers are stocked with almost every organism that a fish might eat. But even these are too unfamiliar for some fish to accept.

I have found that newly imported butterfly fish will sometimes eat fresh clams. Crack the clams open and put the halves in the tank. The odor will attract the fish, and they will start picking away at the clams. Once they start eating this, they can be accustomed to other foods. However, this may not work for specialized feeders such as Moorish idols. They are notoriously difficult to feed in captivity. I've tried to acclimate these fish many times throughout my career

but have always failed miserably. I worked particularly hard with one really nice idol, finally getting it to eat almost everything I offered. Then one day, as I stood admiring it, I decided to go get it some frozen clams to eat. I went to the freezer, got the clams, and thawed them—the whole process took no more than three minutes. But when I got back to the tank, the fish was just lying there, dead. Even though I had been able to trick that fish into eating many different foods, it could not survive on what was for it an unnatural diet. After that, I quit keeping Moorish idols. Other fish I have given up on are pinnatus batfish, blue ribbon eels, and all polyp-eating butterflies. Benefit from my experience and don't try keeping fish that cannot be trained to eat in captivity. In this day and age, it's inhumane to have a pet die from starvation because we *cannot* offer it the foods it would have in its natural habitat.

Don't buy a fish unless you see that it can and will eat in captivity. If you see a fish in a fish store that is not yet eating, don't bring it home until you see it do so. This is one of the drawbacks of buying a fish over the Internet—you can't confirm whether it is eating.

I once knew a man who hated to spend money, even though he had plenty of it. He hunted through numerous pet stores for bargains while always coming to me for free advice. I cheerfully advised him even though I knew he would never spend any money in my store. That was fine with me because he was one of those customers I really didn't want—a constant complainer always wanting to return merchandise.

One day, he came to tell me he had purchased an imperator angelfish, and he had gotten a great deal on it because it wasn't eating. He wanted my advice on what to feed it. I asked him why he assumed it would eat in his tank if it would not eat in the pet store. He seemed confident that he could overcome the problem, and I told him what I could. Every day after that, he came into my store, asking about different foods. Finally, he called me to ask if I would take a look at the fish if he brought it in. The next day at lunchtime, I looked out the window and saw him getting out of his car across the street with a big bag of water. He crossed the westbound lanes of Sunrise Highway and, as he was standing on the divider, the bag broke. Moments later, he rushed into the store with this half-starved fish that had just landed on the hot tarmac and seriously asked me what I could do for it. I told him there was nothing I could do. He then began worrying about his wife berating him for spending so much money on this fish.

There are two lessons you can take away from this sad tale. One, never buy a fish that you haven't seen eat. If it won't eat in the store, it probably won't eat in your home. Two, if you can't afford to lose a $150 fish, buy a $10 fish instead. King Neptune makes no allowances for valuable fish.

How do you get a fish to eat the food you want it to instead of the food it wants to eat?

Fish, like other animals, refuse to eat unfamiliar foods. Although I've prided myself on my ability to get wild-caught fish to eat commercially prepared foods, it's not always an easy (or successful) task. Sometimes it involves feeding the fish a food that it likes bit by bit until it waits for the feeding at the surface of the water. It's even better if there are other fish in the tank to create competition. Drop in a couple of pieces of food that you know the fish likes, then drop in a piece of the food you want it to eat. Most of the time, the fish will snatch it up without realizing that it has eaten an unfamiliar food.

This method works particularly well for fish accustomed to eating live food. Drop one goldfish into the tank, and the fish will grab it; drop in a second goldfish, and it's immediately consumed as well. Then drop in a piece of frozen silverside or freeze-dried krill. As soon as the alternative food hits the water, the fish will snatch it.

In addition, when a fish becomes well acclimated to a tank, it will be more willing to investigate unfamiliar food items. I once had a newly imported adult Achilles tang that refused all foods for three months and became extremely thin. I tried everything, every single day. I became fixated on this fish. I knew the fish wasn't sick. It wasn't eating because it could not find the food it was accustomed to in its native waters of Hawaii. (This is one reason why I don't like to import adult wild-caught fish.)

After three months, this fish finally started eating frozen bloodworms. I have no idea why a fish that lives a hundred feet underwater in Hawaii would decide to eat a freshwater organism such as a bloodworm when it ignored other the fare I thought would be more appealing. But that's what it eventually chose to eat. I fed the Achilles tang small amounts of bloodworms about ten times a day until it began to regain its strength. Then I began adding some misa shrimp, and lo and behold, it started eating those. Day by day, the fish accepted more foods. Now it eats frozen formula foods, pelleted foods, romaine lettuce, and freeze-dried kelp. I was so proud of this accomplishment that I kept this fish, and I still have it several years later.

Are tubifex worms safe, or can they transmit pathogens?

I've fed live tubifex worms to my fish my entire life, and I've never had a case of a fish picking up a pathogen this way. However, I have always rinsed the tubifex worms in running water every day for several days before putting them into the tank. The fish really seem to like them, and they have been an essential food for some of my fish. We used to import kissing goramis from Indonesia, and these fish were not used to eating flakes. If we put tubifex worms into a tubifex worm feeder, they would eat them readily. Later on, they would start eating other foods offered to them. The only fish that I have never been able to wean off of tubifex worms are African arowanas.

However, these days I rarely feed live tubifex worms to my fish because they have become too expensive. Now you can buy so many types of frozen worms that are much more affordable.

With the advent of frozen foods, we can offer our fish much more natural diets at lower cost. For freshwater fish, we have frozen brine shrimp, bloodworms, and mosquito larvae. These are all ready to use, free of parasites, and highly nutritious. And just about any food item found in the ocean is available in a frozen form for marine fish.

Should I stick with one type of food for my fish?

Frozen foods are my preferred choice for fish, but nowadays flake and pellet foods are quite nutritious. They are also very convenient when you are in a hurry and don't have time to thaw frozen food. It is actually a good idea to vary a fish's diet occasionally so that it becomes accustomed to different food sources. If you need to treat your fish for a parasite or infection, it is much easier to dust the medication on flakes or pellets. If your fish are accustomed to eating prepared foods when they are healthy, they will have no hesitation about it when they are ill. As a general rule, it is easier to keep a pet healthy if it will accept a variety of foods. And fish are pets, even if some people seem to think otherwise.

> ### CRACKERS TO CUBES
> When I was a kid, the commercial fish foods available were essentially rice crackers. To keep our fish in good condition, we collected mosquito larvae, daphnia, and tubifex worms from ponds. Or I got beef heart from the butcher and cut that into small pieces for my fish. But as time went on, the formulas of commercial fish foods improved, and freeze-dried worms became available. These came in little cubes that I would squish in the tank. As the cubes absorbed water, the fish eagerly ate them.

I will be away from my tank for about one month and am looking for an automatic fish feeder. Do you have any suggestions?

The best automatic fish feeder is a good friend or relative. I have never placed much faith in automatic fish feeders because most mechanical things in my

When Enough Is Enough

The problem is really not overfeeding the fish as much as it is overfeeding the tank. If you have a hard time limiting the volume of food you put in the tank or don't have the time to ensure that all of the food is consumed before it hits the bottom, you are better off feeding the fish every other day. With the exception of tangs and angelfish, the fish will not starve.

life break at some point. However, if you are going to get an automatic fish feeder, get the best you can afford; cheaper ones will definitely break. As a general rule, you are better off using pelleted rather than flaked food in an automatic feeder. Humidity in the air will cause flaked foods to clump in the automatic feeder and not be dispensed at appropriate times. If you plan to use a pelleted food, make sure that your fish are acclimated to eating it before you go away. Make sure as well that the environment in the house will be OK while you are gone. If the house is going to be locked up for a month with no air-conditioning, it may become as hot as it is outdoors, and you will come home to a tank full of bouillabaisse. If you go away in the winter and turn your heat down to 50 degrees, make sure that you have adequate aquarium heaters to keep the tank warm enough. We don't call them tropical fish for nothing.

How often should you feed fish?

This is a loaded question. Some fish, such as yellow tangs, need to eat continuously; other fish, including lionfish and Oscars, can do fine eating twice a week. I derive great satisfaction from feeding my fish. I try to do it twice a day; sometimes I will feed them as I walk by the tank just to watch them. The idea is to feed them only as much as they will immediately consume. For instance, if you put flakes in the tank, every bit should be eaten in a short amount of time. You can certainly add more after that has been consumed. But it is not advisable to dump a mass of flakes onto the surface of the water so it rains down like snow to the bottom of the tank.

Tangs and angelfish need fresh vegetable matter, such as seaweed, dried kelp, and lettuce, in their diet. So do some other fish; you should make sure to research the needs of your particular fish. It's important to watch as the fish eat vegetable matter because they will rip off pieces that end up floating to the bottom of the tank and rotting there, causing the pH level to drop. In our store, when we put lettuce in our tanks, we always use a net to scoop out any uneaten bits half an hour later. Remember that a fish tank is an enclosed ecosystem—not a lake, pond, or river—and as a result, it will not tolerate much fouling in the way of uneaten food.

How long can fish go without eating?

Fish are opportunistic eaters. Some can go for quite some time without food; others cannot, depending on what type of food they evolved to eat. As a general rule, carnivorous fish can go for extremely long periods without food. A pike, bass, or sunfish goes for months without food during hibernation. But even when they are dormant, they will still eat if the opportunity comes along, as ice fishermen know.

Fish that live in tropical areas and don't hibernate may need to eat continuously. For instance, in their natural state, tangs continuously consume algae off of rocks. There is nothing more pathetic than a yellow or purple tang in an aquarium with a sunken stomach, lateral line disease, and washed-out color because it has been underfed. A wild-caught fish such as this might eat flakes three times a day, but that still won't be enough. It has evolved to eat large quantities of high-fiber food, and it needs the same diet in captivity. Such fish need lettuce, kelp, spirulina, and other vegetation to remain healthy. We should choose fish that fit our lifestyles. If you don't have time to feed a high-maintenance saltwater fish such as a tang, then keep predatory fish such as moray eels and lionfish. These can easily go for a few days without being fed.

How long should you leave fruits and vegetables (used as fish food) in an aquarium?

In my store, we feed our saltwater fish lettuce and kelp daily. We only leave it in the tanks for about half an hour. Pieces of lettuce will break off and settle in corners of the tank, reducing the pH level of the water. We also feed zucchini sticks and dried peas to our plecos at night as soon as we shut off the lights. First thing in the morning, we remove any leftovers. Zucchini sticks are easier to find. Peas can be scattered all about the tank. We feed goldfish frozen corn and peas; that doesn't cause a problem because they consume it all immediately. But as a rule, any type of organic material should remain in your tank for as short a time as possible.

I have some fish food that's been stored in my home in a dry closet for about four years. I have some old freeze-dried bloodworms and some old betta pellets. Are these foods still good?

These old foods wouldn't hurt the fish, but I am sure that after all this time they have lost most of their nutritional value. Most freeze-dried and prepared fish foods are fairly inexpensive; quite frankly, I would just throw them out and replace them.

How important are live foods for aquarium fish these days?

When I was a kid, live food was sometimes all we had to feed our fish. As I have mentioned before, the flaked foods available then were basically nothing more than rice crackers. To keep our fish in good condition, we had to collect live food for them. We made nets from curtains and scooped up daphnia and mosquito larvae from puddles and ponds in the woods. The freshwater organisms that I collected for my fish were quite fascinating, and I sometimes set up little tanks so that I could study them. I was probably the only kid who devoted time to observing the entire life cycle of the mosquito. I also hatched brine shrimp from eggs that I bought at the pet store. We fed the baker's yeast to the brine shrimp so they would grow and make better meals for the fish. We also collected earthworms and kept them in boxes in our attics so that the fish would have live food during the winter.

But the advent of frozen and prepared fish foods has made this unnecessary. When I gathered these live foods for my fish, I was assured of their nutritional value. But many of the commercial live foods sold in pet stores, such as black worms and tubifex worms, are collected from extremely polluted water. They must be kept in fresh water for several days in order to cleanse them of impurities. I rarely feed my fish any live foods these days. Almost every fish will accept frozen fish foods if trained to eat them.

Do feeder fish such as guppies have much nutritional value, and should they be used as the main staple of a fish's diet?

The topic of using live fish to feed other fish is somewhat controversial. I personally only do this for newly imported fish that are strict fish eaters, such as some kinds of gars, wrasses, and freshwater barracudas. However, animals that eat live prey can be weaned to prepared foods. I've done this with birds, snakes, and fish. Feeder fish like guppies and goldfish that are used for food in a home aquarium are often raised and housed in horribly filthy conditions. Why would you want to put these compromised fish in your home aquarium? There is no telling what kind of parasites they might introduce.

It's true that some fish will only eat live fish when you first get them. But once they become acclimated and tame and understand when they will be fed, they become more willing to accept other foods. For instance, if you drop orange goldfish one at a time into a tank of eagerly awaiting gars, they will snatch them immediately. After giving them a couple of goldfish, drop an orange piece of freeze-dried krill into the tank. The waiting gars will eagerly grab anything that splashes into the water, including the krill. Frozen fish can also be used for this. Drop one or two live fish into the tank, and then alternate the live fish with a frozen fish. Fish are pets and, just like any other pet, they can learn via positive reinforcement.

If you want to feed live fish, set up a separate tank at home in which to keep the feeder fish. This tank should have a high level of copper to kill any parasites. Plus, caring for the fish for a few weeks will ensure that they are stronger and healthier and have a higher nutritional value. However, high copper concentrations in the fish may become an issue if these fish were fed to an invertebrate like an octopus. Invertebrates cannot handle copper at all.

Water Quality Perfection

Many years ago, a German watchmaker who had just moved to the United States came into my store to buy a 150-gallon tank and two 30-gallon tanks. He had kept marine fish in Germany and wanted to resume his hobby. As he explained to me later, once he got home with his tanks, he set up the 150-gallon tank with an undergravel filter, canister filter, and ultraviolet light sterilizer. This part of his setup was fairly standard; what was unique was the rest of it. Next, he drilled holes in the 30-gallon tanks to attach one to the left side and one to the right side of the 150-gallon tank. He connected the three tanks with PVC pipe and a ball valve.

He kept both 30-gallon tanks full of newly mixed salt water, filtered by a small canister filter. Each day, he opened the ball valve on either the right or the left, thus connecting the large tank with one of the small ones. So the fish actually had a 180-gallon environment. Each day, he drained the water from the 30-gallon tank that he wasn't using and

refilled it to prepare for the next day's water change. He was able to change 30 gallons daily by opening the valve and connecting the two tanks, which prevented any stress to the fish. The water flowed and mixed together just as it would in an ocean. The results were astounding. He bought a baby saddleback butterfly from me and a baby copperband butterfly, fish normally hard to keep alive. They grew to be 12 inches long after one year in this tank. He also fed the fish eight times a day, which he could do because he kept the tank in his workshop and fed the fish small bits of different foods throughout the day. Obviously, you would not be able to do this in any other type of tank. Feeding the fish that often would rapidly pollute the water. But he changed the water every day, so it was never a problem. I never saw such perfect fish. This certainly illustrates the importance of water quality.

What is the difference between *cycling* a saltwater tank and *establishing* a saltwater tank?

The phrase "cycling a saltwater tank" is rather ambiguous. This process establishes populations of bacteria that will convert toxic fish waste into less toxic fish waste. In reality, the same process occurs when you cycle and establish a tank. This needs to be done in any fish tank or pond, whether it's a saltwater tank, a freshwater tank, or an outdoor garden pond. The process gets more attention in saltwater tanks because we don't even notice it taking place in freshwater tanks.

It's very simple. If there is something to be eaten in any environment, something else will move into that niche to eat it. There are different types of bacteria that consume two types of chemicals. One consumes ammonia, and the other consumes nitrite. These bacteria exist everywhere in a dormant state. They come to life in any aquatic environment full of oxygen with some amount of ammonia and nitrite.

When we fill a fish tank with water and add filtration and fish, we provide this environment. Fish urine in the water adds ammonia; however, ammonia is toxic to the fish if they are exposed to it for long periods. Fortunately, this environment is conducive to the bacteria, which become active and consume the ammonia as fast as the fish produce it. Unfortunately, the bacteria convert that ammonia into equally toxic nitrite. Once the tank becomes full of nitrite, another type of bacteria will become active to consume the nitrite and produce less toxic chemicals called nitrates, which are only harmful to fish in extremely large concentrations.

This process, called a cycle, usually takes six to nine weeks in a saltwater aquarium. First, the fish produces ammonia; next, the bacteria consume the ammonia and convert it into nitrite; finally, bacteria consume the nitrite and convert this into nitrate. In a freshwater tank, the process takes about four weeks.

> ### FISHLESS CYCLING
> In a fishless cycle, pure ammonia is added to the aquarium to start the growth of ammonia- and nitrite-consuming bacteria. When you add that first inoculation of ammonia into the tank, it starts the cycle and bacteria grow to consume it. However, when you use fish to create a cycle, a new inoculation of ammonia is produced every day. A fishless cycle lacks this natural daily production of ammonia; it's a one-shot deal. Perhaps this is the problem I've had with this method. Some people have had great success with the process, but I never have.

How often should people perform water changes, and what volume of water should be swapped out?

Back in the 1960s, changing water in an aquarium was considered bad. When we siphoned off organic matter from the bottom of the tank, we collected the water in a bucket, strained it through a piece of cheesecloth, and poured it back into the tank. The water in these tanks became so old that it eventually turned yellow. We thought that was a good thing and described these tanks as "well aged." It's amazing that the fish adapted to this kind of water chemistry (not all did, of course; some died). Of course, back then most of us did not keep many fish in the tank, or many delicate fish, because we had limited funds to devote to this hobby.

Views on this subject have changed completely, and frequent water changes are now encouraged. Small water changes are also considered superior to large ones. They are also much easier. In a 20-gallon tank, it's easy to get a 1-gallon water bottle, draw off 2 gallons, and replace it. But changing 5 gallons involves a big bucket, a siphon hose, sloshing a big bucket of dirty water through the house as your spouse or housemate yells at you, and trying to tilt a 5-gallon bucket back into the tank without spilling it while your housemate hovers around with paper towels and a mop. Small, frequent water changes are far better. I like to change about 10 percent of the water once a week. Even if you change only 2 or 5 percent of the water, 50 percent of something is better than 100 percent of nothing.

Why haven't more people embraced fishless cycling as the way to go? Can't it be just as dangerous to dump a bunch of fish into a fishless cycled tank as it is to cycle with fish?

Cycling a tank with pure ammonia has not worked very well for me, but it has worked for other people and perhaps it will work for you. Smart fish keepers will take advantage of new methods and ideas. However, very few aquarists enjoy watching an empty tank for eight weeks, which is the time it usually takes to cycle a tank. Even if you use only a panther, coney, red hind, or miniatus grouper or a moray eel to cycle your tank, it gives you something to feed and look at for those weeks, and that is what pet keeping is all about. Years ago, we used damsel fish to cycle tanks, but an eel or a grouper is a better choice for two reasons. First, they are both larger than damsel fish. Second, once the tank is cycled it is nearly impossible to catch damsel fish to remove them from the tank. You practically have to dismantle the tank to get them out because they swim so fast.

A responsible pet keeper will only cycle a tank with fish that can endure the process. No one wants to dump fish into a brand-new tank and simply let them take their chances. We have a few groupers in our store that we have lent out to customers for years to cycle new tanks. After the tank is cycled, the customers bring the groupers back, they get the fish they want, and the groupers go on to cycle other tanks. This hasn't done the groupers any harm.

What's the difference in the time it takes to fishless cycle versus cycling with fish?

The reason why a fishless cycle seems to take less time is probably because all of the ammonia is added at once. Therefore, only a finite amount of ammonia must be transformed into nitrites, and a finite amount of nitrites must be transformed into nitrates by the aerobic bacteria colonizing the tank. When cycling a tank with fish, ammonia is continuously added to the water, so it takes much longer for the colonizing bacteria to get this under control. However, the fishless cycle will not produce a bacteria bed that is as strong and populous as that produced with fish. In my experience, it takes six to twelve weeks to cycle a tank naturally. A fishless cycle may take half that time. But the fishless cycle will produce a smaller bacteria bed, so you will need to stock the tank much more slowly.

I've heard that people fishless cycle their tanks with substances other than ammonia. I know fish food tends to break down into ammonia by itself, but how does the process work with brown sugar or a dead shrimp?

The goal of cycling a tank is to grow a bacteria bed that will consume the ammonia produced by the fish in the water. The best medium to grow these bacteria will be produced by fish or other aquatic organisms. Many aquatic organisms can be used to do this naturally, so I really don't see the need for alternatives such as brown sugar or dead shrimp. Yes, the bacteria may consume the secondhand ammonia produced by cycling substitutes, but the

objective is to grow bacteria that will consume the ammonia in fish urine, which is different.

When we set up tanks back in the 1960s, no one had any idea about the nitrogen cycle. Most of us didn't have the money to put a lot of fish in the tank. We bought two or three fish and collected cans for a few weeks to raise more money. The few fish in the tank during that time produced just enough ammonia to cycle the tank without killing the fish. By that time, we had saved up the money to buy a few more fish. We had no idea that we were actually cycling the tank during these weeks.

Nowadays, people tend to be able to add more fish to a new tank more quickly. As a result, we must pay closer attention to cycling the tank.

Will heavy use of chlorine remover oversalt the tank? Could there be a buildup of enough salt to harm the fish?

Although chlorine remover is a sodium product (sodium thiophosphate), its use, in my experience, is not much of a problem. Freshwater fish can tolerate a certain level of salt. I always add aquarium salt to the water to make it a little denser anyway. The only time using a chlorine remover may be an issue is in a heavily planted tank where you don't want any salt at all. However, with planted tanks, you don't need to worry about sodium thiophosphate. When you do a water change in a heavily planted tank, you can use bottled water anyway; there is no chlorine in bottled water.

How often should I test my nitrate, nitrite, ammonia, and pH?

The ammonia level fluctuates throughout the day, depending on the biological situation in the tank at any given time. It will be affected by actions such as feeding the fish. You may check the level at noon and find it high. Check it again three hours later, and it may be normal. This is a result of the action of the bacteria in the tank. At my store, we test all of our tanks every day because their pH constantly drops. We check the nitrite levels every day because these can also fluctuate. There will be times when the level is high and times when it is low. In most established aquariums, nitrate levels always seem to be high no matter how often you do a water change. But as I said before, nitrates are not as toxic as ammonia and nitrites are. In a fish-only tank, it is really not an issue. In invertebrate and reef tanks, excess nitrates can pose a problem.

It's up to you as a fish keeper to maintain optimum water quality in your tank. If you check the water frequently, you will have a better understanding of the typical environment in your tank. Your fish are dependent on you for this. They can't test the water themselves. If the water quality is bad, the only way they can let you know is by dying.

Why would the pH of a tank drop suddenly in only one day?

Many things can cause pH to drop quickly, especially a rapid influx of organic material. Overfeeding can result in a combination of uneaten food and excess fish waste from overeating. If you give your fish pieces of lettuce and don't remove the uneaten lettuce after an hour, this organic matter can also cause a rapid drop in the pH. Adding a lot of new fish to the tank can make the pH level drop. Using water with a lower pH for a water change can also do it. That's why every aquarist should have a pH test kit in his or her arsenal of tools.

How do you alter pH? What do you do if you have very high pH? Or very low pH?

The letters *pH* stand for the percentage of hydrogen ions in the aquarium. This percentage varies. When the percentage of hydrogen ions is low, the water is considered acid; if the percentage is high, the water is considered alkaline. We've all heard of acid rain. In upstate New York, a lot of the fish that were native to the region died out because the acid rain has lowered the pH of the ponds and lakes to the point where fish cannot thrive. More organic material in a tank causes the pH to drop faster. Minerals and carbonates that dissolve in the water cause the pH to stay higher. A shallow pond or river containing lots of leaves and other organic material will have a very low pH.

Every body of water with a natural pH level contains fish that are adapted to this. Discus and cardinal tetras that evolved in Amazonian rivers with a very low pH need the same low pH in fish tanks. Conversely, African cichlids evolved in the rift lakes of Africa, so they are naturally adapted to a very high pH level.

An aquarium is a glass box in a living room, full of organic material such as fish waste, dirty filter media, and uneaten food. This organic matter will constantly lower the pH level. It is the fish keeper's responsibility to test the pH level every week and use the appropriate chemicals to bring it to the proper level for the particular fish in that tank. To raise the pH, we generally use sodium bicarbonate, and to lower it, we use sodium biphosphate.

Is there any other way to lower pH? I've tried the 7.0 pH buffer and a Wardley buffer, but the pH still won't go down.

Automatic pH buffers don't work as well as the manufacturers claim. And I never really understood how these buffering agents could work when I don't even know how much buffering agent to add to get an aquarium to precisely the right level for the fish in that tank. These buffering agents must perform well in some tanks; otherwise, they would not be for sale. But what goes on in a laboratory setting is not quite the same as what goes on in a home aquarium.

> **TIME AND pH**
> Time will lower pH naturally in any enclosed body of water without access to mineral salts. Some liquid pH-reducing formulas contain sulfuric acid. Just saying *sulfuric acid* is kind of scary to me, let alone pouring some into my fish tank.

The best way to handle the issue of pH is to test the water manually with a pH test kit and use sodium bicarbonate to raise the pH or sodium biphosphate to lower it. To lower the pH, add small amounts of sodium biphospate to the water for a couple of days, testing as you go to make sure you don't lower it too quickly. Once you add enough sodium biphosphate, the pH will go down to the desired level.

After my local fish store tested my water, they soaked my glass test vials in salt water to clean off any chemical residue. Is this necessary?

I rinse my vials with very hot water and let them air dry. When I was a kid, I worked at a fish wholesaler. There was always a coffee pot full of water, boiling away. We used to soak our nets before using them in different tanks. That killed anything that could have been transferred from one tank to another.

What are the various causes of cloudy water?

If your water was clear and is now hazy, the first thing to consider is the possibility of an ammonia bloom in the tank. New tanks that become hazy always have ammonia in them, but this can also develop in an older, established tank if the filter is compromised.

If you test the ammonia level and this isn't the problem, you then know the filter is compromised and is no longer keeping the water as clean as it should. There can be several reasons for this. It may be dirty, or it may be broken and not filtering a normal volume of water. Perhaps you have added more fish to the tank than the filter can handle, or the fish have grown larger than the filter can handle.

If there is too much ammonia in the tank, you should examine these same possibilities. The filter may have been fine in February, but your fish have been growing and now they are producing more waste products. Therefore, the filter may not have enough room to grow enough bacteria to handle this increased load of biological waste.

The solution is to put a bigger filter on the tank or add an additional filter. The filter has to handle the fish load. This is where the term *balanced aquarium* came from many years ago. Filtration is all about balance.

How do I test the water in all of my tanks without risking contamination? Do I use a separate master test kit for each tank? Do I use separate sets of testing vials for each tank?

This depends on how many tanks you have. In most home settings, people don't have that many aquariums, and the fish population remains relatively stable. It's also pretty obvious when you have a problem in one of your tanks. If you are worried about contamination issues, rinse the glass vials with very hot water and allow them to air dry; this process will kill any pathogens found in a home aquarium. If you are really concerned, it's not a big deal to purchase some extra vials and have a separate set for each tank.

Do water parameter test kits expire? How long are they usually good for?

Like any chemical compound, testing kit materials can break down over time. But the kits sold in most pet shops are so small, and any good aquarist will test his or her water frequently enough to use up a package of these reactants long before they expire.

Are test strips or liquid test kits better?

I've tried test strips, but I really don't trust them because I am not sure what sort of contaminants may be on them. I've always been happy with liquid or powder reactants. They are affordable and accurate, so I don't see a reason to use anything else. But try them all and discover what works best for you.

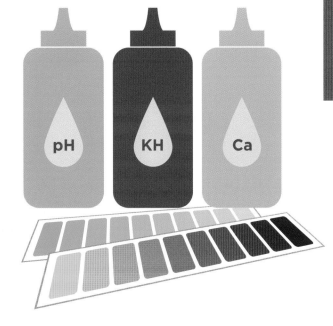

Can smelling the tank water tip you off to problems? Are there different smells associated with the tank conditions?

If the concentration is high enough, I can smell ammonia in a tank. But the water usually develops a white haze when the level is that high. This should tip you off well before you notice any odor. Otherwise, I have never been able to gauge water quality by smelling it, and my sense of smell is extremely acute. To me, water with a low pH level smells exactly the same as water with a high pH. Salt water smells distinctly different from fresh water, and a reef tank will smell different from a fish-only saltwater tank. These differences become more noticeable as you gain experience keeping different types of fish, but I would never consider this as a reliable indicator of water quality or possible water chemistry problems.

Supersize Fish Tanks

Extremes characterize the professional fish keeping that I do. One minute I am putting together a small fishbowl with one betta for a small child, and the next I find myself working on a 500-gallon reef tank for a restaurant. But the largest setup I ever undertook was for an art dealer in midtown Manhattan. He had a swimming pool in the basement of his townhouse and wanted a fish tank to wrap around the back and one side of the pool. He originally wanted one big tank, but it was impossible to get such large pieces of glass in there in one piece. The tanks had to be constructed on-site. We installed three saltwater tanks along the long side of the pool and two freshwater tanks along the short side. Because the client didn't want to hear running water, we had to install the filters in the floor below. The structural and engineering aspects were complicated but doable.

It took about two weeks to construct the tanks. Once they were finished, I cycled them all and then had the fun of choosing fish for them. Trusting me completely, the homeowner, an ardent conservationist, left it to me to decide which fish would thrive best in those tanks. He only wanted fish that would thrive in captivity.

In the first saltwater tank, the predator tank, I had small bamboo and cat sharks living on the bottom. These are the only sharks that will thrive and breed in a home aquarium, albeit a very large one. In the top part of the tank were six large lionfish. In the middle saltwater tank, I placed naso and sohal tangs, permits or lookdowns, red snappers, two large beautiful panther groupers, and a tiera batfish. All of these will grow and thrive in captivity if fed the right diet. In the third saltwater tank, I made an artificial reef from resin and filled it with tank-bred percula clowns, saddle clowns, tomato clowns, and a few blue and domino damsels. All of these also do well in captivity.

In the first freshwater tank, I put tinfoil barbs, silver dollars, red parrotfish, and a couple of soft-shell turtles. They all got along nicely. The fish were too large for the turtles to bother, and the turtles were a big hit. The homeowner wanted the other freshwater tank to be a planted tank with small fish such as cardinal and neon tetras. However, it is difficult for small fish to eat in a 5-foot-deep tank, and the current was really too strong for them. It is also hard to illuminate a tank that deep to provide enough lights for plants without intense algae growth on the glass. I planted java fern on the bottom of the tank because it doesn't need that much light. I also planted crinums, or onion plants, which grew all the way to the surface of the tank, to provide the desired effect. Then I added giant danios, a huge school of tiger barbs of every color, and some colorful plecostomus catfish to keep things clean.

Maintaining those tanks was a true pleasure, and it was one of the few times when I had full control over a customer's tank. The homeowner was very pleased, and those tanks were there for fifteen years. Of course, not all fish live that long, so we regularly removed and added fish. Nothing lasts forever. The owner eventually got divorced and moved. At the same time, someone bought the house next door and knocked it down. The resulting vibrations caused the tanks to break. That was a big mess, and the end of those five beautiful giant aquariums. The fish fell into the swimming pool, and only the freshwater fish survived. It was a real pet disaster.

How much weight can a floor support, and how can you check to be sure it will support a large aquarium?

Water weighs slightly more than 8 pounds per gallon. Even a 10-gallon fish tank will weigh 80 pounds in addition to its stand. If you want to put a really big tank in your house—a 300-gallon one, for instance, which will weigh some 2,400 pounds—you need to discover whether your floor will support it. First, measure the space between the studs below the floor, and then talk to an engineer about whether those studs and that spacing can safely support the weight. If you live in an apartment building, the superintendent can usually answer that question. If you live in a private house, you will need to consult an architect or engineer.

The largest aquariums I ever set up in New York City were the five 500-gallon tanks I described earlier. The engineers I spoke with said that the weight would be no issue at all because of the studs and spacing in the design of the building. The biggest problem encountered was that the tanks were so large that we could not get them into the building. None of the doors or hallways was wide enough. As I said, we had to carry in the glass and build the tanks on-site.

What is a safe way to level a tank?

When leveling tanks, the entire base must be level. If the tank is on a wrought-iron stand, it only comes into contact with the edges of the aquarium. If the floor is crooked and you even this out by putting shims under the legs, it may still place pressure on the floor of the tank. For small tanks up to 30 gallons, this probably won't be an issue. But if I set up a large tank on a wrought-iron stand and the floor is not level, I always cut a piece of plywood the exact size of the tank and place that under the tank itself. This ensures that the weight of the tank is evenly distributed. Then we shim the stand so that everything is totally level.

I've been interested in building a coffee-table aquarium, but would it stress the fish to have people putting glasses on top of the tank, playing games on it, and constantly walking by?

With the right conditions inside the tank, fish can get used to just about anything that normally occurs outside the tank. The water quality must be good, and the fish must have suitable hiding places in the tank. The problem with coffee-table tanks is keeping them clean. Algae quickly grow on the underside of the top, which is the table's surface. The tank becomes such a mess of algae that it cannot be cleaned properly. I've been asked to set up this type of tank for customers, and then just months later I'm asked to take it down. It would probably work better if you set up a fishless tank, using underwater lighting and bubbles to create visual interest rather than using live fish. That way, you could keep a small amount of chlorine bleach in the water to prevent algae.

My fish tank is leaking. I went to the pet store, but the silicone glue they sell there is five times the price of a tube of silicone at the hardware store. Can I use that instead?

No, definitely not. The silicone sold in pet shops to repair aquariums is pure silicone. Similar products sold in hardware stores to caulk tile and windows usually have antifungal ingredients added to them.

When you repair your aquarium, the area must be totally dry. Scrape off the old silicone and clean it thoroughly to ensure that you get a tight seal. The biggest problem is recommended curing time. The package usually says "dries in half an hour but allow two days to cure," but nobody wants to wait two days, so they put the water in too soon and compromise the new seal. If the directions tell you to wait two days, do it. However, I must confess that I have not always followed this rule myself. Situations have come up when large aquariums were leaking in office buildings or at the home of someone planning a big dinner party that night. We have refilled the tanks after letting the silicone set for only an hour or two, and

HIDING THE EQUIPMENT
For those who prefer to keep as much of the equipment and plugs on their tanks out of view as possible, there are various ways to go about it. Today we can drill glass and add bulkhead fittings and PVC drains to tanks. It is a simple matter to arrange filtration, intakes, and out-takes for those tanks. An electrician can always put an electrical box under the tank to keep the wires hidden.

these tanks have not leaked. But I still recommend that you stick with the silicone manufacturers' guidelines to be safe.

All other glues on the market cannot be considered safe for aquariums except for PVC glue. The innovations of PVC and PVC glue have led to a new era of aquarium keeping. We can now drill holes in tanks, apply bulkhead fittings, and connect tanks together to make the vast central systems that have become so popular.

I want to move my tank to a room that I am setting up for my reflexology and massage business. Will it be OK for me to burn oils and candles in the room?

Residual smoke in these situations is minor. Assuming that your tank is covered, I doubt that any residue could get into the tank to cause problems for the fish. Extremely strong scents or fragrances in the room could be sucked into the tank via an air pump. This forced contact with the water has the potential to compromise the water quality, but I seriously doubt that anything you might use in this situation could harm the fish in any way, shape, or form.

Does the ammonia version of the fishless cycle hurt live plants?

Technically, it should not hurt live plants because many of them feed off of ammonia. However, it does depend on the level of ammonia in the water. When a dog pees on a lawn, the high ammonia concentration in the center of the pee spot kills the grass. But the lower concentrations around the edges act as fertilizer. That grass around the stain will consequently be much lusher and greener than the rest of the lawn. The same rule applies when you add chemical ammonia to a fishless tank to cycle it. If the concentration is too high, the plants will die. If it is low, the plants will thrive. This is something you must gauge through trial and error.

Years ago, I did fishless cycles using concentrated ammonia. I never found this method to be as good as putting a few hardy fish in the tank and letting the process occur naturally.

How much light do aquarium plants need?

Plants definitely need lots of light. Plants grown for the aquarium trade are propagated in greenhouses with shallow water and full sun. Most of them wither away if they are placed in a home aquarium in a dark corner of the living room with a single fluorescent bulb for light.

The amount of sunlight that each plant needs depends on the plants, the location of the tank, and plain old luck. When I was a child, we didn't have gro lights, only incandescent bulbs, for fish tanks. Even with those, the plants did reasonably well. Today, there are many different types and strengths of bulbs on the market. As a rule, cheaper ones are much less efficient at simulating natural sunlight. Expensive bulbs are much closer to natural sunlight.

You can find a spectrum analysis printed on the package of every lightbulb sold in pet shops. My advice is to get the best one you can afford. Halide bulbs seem to produce the best plant growth, but they are very expensive and use lots of electricity.

NO FISH NEEDED

Plants need light; everything else, including fish, is optional. For the most part, fish compromise tanks with plants. The only fish that are beneficial to aquatic plants are some of the smaller algae-eating catfish such as otocinclus catfish. These fish will clean hair algae from the leaves of aquatic plants.

Do plants need a current, water changes, and/or a filter?

Strong currents compromise plants, which is why you don't find them growing in fast-moving rivers. However, some filtration is necessary to prevent the water from becoming stagnant. Years ago, we kept balanced aquariums. These were 10- or 20-gallon aquariums with live plants, three or four fish, and no filtration at all. The plants added oxygen to the water. Supposedly, the fish produced carbon dioxide, which helped the plants. It was a little aquatic utopia.

A few years ago, I decided to make one of these balanced aquariums in a 55-gallon tank. I set it up with plants, filled it with water, and left it with a strong light so that the plants could grow before I added the fish. I intended to add some small fish such as zebra danios, white cloud mountain minnows, and otocinclus catfish. To my surprise, when I checked the tank two weeks later, I found tiny fry fish swimming around. The eggs must have been on the plants that I ordered from Florida. I left everything alone, and those fry grew up to be some species of dace that I could never quite identify. Eventually, I did put a filter on this tank because after a couple of months the surface developed scum even though the water always smelled fine. You have to realize that an environment like this is totally unnatural. The surface of any outdoor body of water is constantly broken by wind and rain, and some kind of water exchange always occurs in nature.

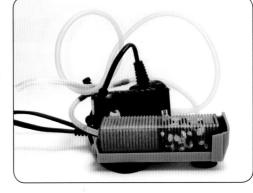

Do plants need a pump with oxygen?

Plants do better with carbon dioxide in the water, and you can place a carbon dioxide reactor in the aquarium. However, in my experience, additional carbon dioxide encourages the plants to grow way too big, way too fast. You must then spend most of the time trimming, pruning, cutting, and dividing them. In the average home aquarium, you don't want the plants to grow too much, so a carbon dioxide reactor is not necessary.

I'm looking to move about a half an hour away. What's the best way to go about relocating an aquarium that has live plants?

The best way to transport live plants is to remove them from the tank and wrap each one individually in very wet newspaper. This protects them from breakage. Plants placed inside a bag full of water can be shaken apart, and the stems can be weakened or broken. Transported in wet newspaper, the plants arrive at their destination in one piece. As long as the newspaper is sufficiently wet, they can easily remain out of water for a day. This is how aquatic plants are shipped all over the world.

Should I quarantine plants before adding them to a tank? Can they give other plants diseases or carry anything (e.g., snail eggs) that could hurt the fish ?

Little pond snails are probably the only noxious problem that could be transmitted by plants. If you want to ensure that your plants are free of viable pond snail eggs, fill a bucket with water, then add some freshwater ich medication containing copper. Use twice the recommended dose, and leave the plants in this solution for two days. The copper will kill any snail eggs that might be lurking there. This method is safe for just about any type of plant. Rinse the plants well before putting them in your fish tank. They should be as sterile as any live plant can possibly be. If you want something completely sterile, use plastic plants.

I recently had hair algae growing on the edges of my live plants. Is there a way to remove it that won't hurt the plants?

Hair algae has been a bane of my life. It rarely goes away on its own, and only a very few fish, such the otocinclus catfish, will eat it. If the live plants in your tank grow aggressively enough, they will outgrow the hair algae. But if they are compromised, the hair algae beats them to the punch. In your situation, the best approach is to pull out the plants and use your fingers to gently remove the algae from the edges of the leaves. This will not harm the plants. However, hair algae is very difficult to remove from bunch plants such as cabomba and hornwort. You are better off discarding those plants and buying new ones.

Are banana plants difficult to keep? Do they need CO_2 or fertilizers?

Banana plants, which have always been one of my favorites for a freshwater tank, get their name from their roots. When you buy one in the pet store, it's generally a bit of root shaped like a bunch of bananas with a couple of green leaves. In an ideal situation, banana plants will grow to the surface and float there, like water lilies, producing delightful little flowers. Banana plants do best in shallow water where their leaves can reach the surface. If you really want to grow them, they should be put into soil rather than directly into the gravel in an aquarium. Begin by filling a little jar or glass with clean soil and covering the top layer with a half inch of gravel. Then stick the container into a bucket of water for about a week so that the excess free-floating dirt can get wet and settle. After a week, take the jar out and bury the banana plant in the gravel so that the tips of the thick roots are touching the soil. Place the jar and plant in an aquarium with about 8 inches of water and bright lights. You will be pleasantly surprised at how well it grows under these conditions.

I have not found carbon dioxide additions or fertilizers are necessary when banana plants are properly planted at the correct water depth with sufficient light.

How do I get my anubias plant to vegetatively propagate?

Anubias are not the hardiest freshwater plants. They look beautiful when we buy them, but they are grown in greenhouses in shallow water and full sunlight, with no fish or strong currents. When placed in deep tanks with fish, they

slowly die. With anubias or any other plant, be sure to have the right amount of light—as already stated, proper lighting is the most important thing for any aquatic plant. A single bulb over a tank in a living room with no natural light will not be sufficient. I have, however, grown some of my best plants in a tank with one bulb in front of a sunny window. (There should only be plants in this tank, no fish.)

It's also important to know where a plant was grown before you got it so that you can duplicate those conditions. Whenever possible, try to get plants propagated in hobbyist aquariums. Those plants always do the best because they are acclimated to the environment of a home aquarium. (This is also true of fish that are raised in a home aquarium.) One reason that fish clubs are so cool is that you can trade cuttings of aquarium plants with other club members.

In a planted tank, why would only one species of plant be dying off while all the others are thriving?

Like terrestrial plants, different aquatic plants have different requirements, including lighting and water chemistry. In addition, some of the aquatic plants sold in pet shops are not true aquatic plants. They are actually bog plants or house plants that die very slowly when kept underwater. So when you go to buy plants, make sure to ask whether they are true aquatics. Find out the amount of light the plants need, too, and the best water depth for them. For instance, Java ferns prefer a lower light level than many other plants do. Banana plants prefer shallow rather than deep water. Certain plants will do OK in high currents; others must have no currents. To make sure it is a success, an aquatic garden should be given the same kind of forethought and planning that you would give a terrestrial garden. It's a matter of choosing the right plants for your garden.

I have some artificial plants in my aquarium that are starting to get a reddish-brown gunk buildup. Any ideas on how to clean the plants? Should I boil them?

Boiling will remove the gunk, but it will also discolor the plants. As a general rule, if the plants have big, thick green leaves, this kind of buildup can be wiped off with a coarse sponge. If they are imitations of fine-leafed plants such as cabomba or hornwort, fill a bucket with water, add four or five tablespoons of bleach, and submerge the plants for an hour. They should look brand-new afterward. If they do not, add another tablespoon of bleach and wait another hour. When you take the plants out of the bucket, run them under cold water for a good half hour to remove any residue of bleach. The plants will be nice and clean, and the bleach will not damage the plastic as boiling would.

A local fish store employee suggested that I use barley extract for an algae problem in my 95-gallon tank. I guess it is normally used in ponds, but he said he had been using it in his home aquarium with success. What do you think?

I have never had much success with the barley method to control algae in fish ponds or aquariums. I am a strong proponent of ultraviolet light sterilization. The key to using barley extract is to closely monitor the pH level to ensure that it doesn't drop too drastically. Barley works well in a pond because the volume of water is much greater. Plus, the goldfish and koi kept in ponds are far more resistant to rapid fluctuations in pH levels compared with tropical fish in a 55-gallon aquarium. I never encountered an algae problem in a home aquarium that did not respond to ultraviolet light sterilization.

I'm in the process of converting my 55-gallon tank into a reef. Do I need a calcium reactor? What are the pros and the cons?

Reef tanks can be as simple or complicated as you like. If you like to tinker with gadgets, the technology

FISH FOOD GOING TO THE DOGS

Don't assume that your dog can't smell the fish food in a sealed container just because you don't notice it. Many fish keepers store their food in a cabinet beneath the fish tank. Dogs typically find it very easy to open these doors and help themselves to a fish-food snack. Over the years, my dogs have always sought out containers of fish food. They take them to a quiet corner of the house, crack them open with their back teeth, and spend a delightful hour licking up fish-food flakes. This has happened to me more times than I can count.

available for reef tanks stretches from here to eternity—calcium reactors, redux meters, reverse osmosis filters, and so on and so on. Each piece of equipment has its own purpose, and whether you need a particular piece depends on what type of animals you plan to keep. If you plan to have a reef tank of soft corals, crustaceans, and small fish, for instance, the calcium level is not so important, so a calcium reactor is not necessary. Calcium is very important, however, in a reef tank containing stony corals and coralline algae. Although stony corals such as acropora may not look like live animals, they are, and they deserve the best possible care you can give them. Any technology that you can buy to maintain proper calcium levels, including a calcium reactor, will be to their advantage—as long as you can afford it.

Of course, every time I state that certain technology is necessary, I always hear from someone who has successfully managed without it for years. But not every fish keeper is that lucky.

How long does it take for sand to settle in a tank? Is the settling sand bad for the fish?

In my opinion, it's not a good idea to put the fish in a home aquarium until the sand is totally settled and the water is clear. If the water is murky because of a lot of free-floating sand, this is uncomfortable for the fish. The sand particles entering their mouths and exiting their gills would be comparable to you breathing air filled with dust. Whether this causes long-term damage to the fish is debatable. In nature, fish experience these situations every time a hard rainstorm stirs up silt and sand in the water. However, it's never a good idea to make comparisons between fish in a home aquarium and their wild counterparts. Home-aquarium fish are usually compromised to some extent for one reason or another.

How do you clean coral sand?

When I was a kid, we used builder's sand or playground sand in our aquariums. We would put it into a bucket in the driveway, stick a hose in, and pay my little brother a nickel to stand there and stir it with a stick for an hour. All of the organic matter and other impurities were washed away as the water flowed up and out of the bucket, down the driveway, and into the gutter. Meanwhile, the bigger kids would have a great time floating little paper sailboats in the gutter and throwing mud at each other while my poor little brother was stuck stirring sand.

This method is the best way to ensure that the sand is perfectly clean, and I still use it (sans brother) even though the bags of sand sold in my pet store are prewashed. Run fresh water through the sand and stir until the water in the bucket is totally clear.

What do you do for your fish tank when the power goes out? How to you regulate the water temperature?

This depends on the size of the tank, the number of fish, and the ambient temperature of the room. If this happens in March or April and the room isn't too cold, the fish could survive much longer than they would during a power outage in July or January. If you lose power during a hot summer day, the temperature in the tank will lock up at whatever the air temperature happens to be, which could be 100 degrees. If it happens in winter, it could drop low enough for the water to freeze.

In hot weather, you can place bags of ice in the water to cool it. Do not drop ice cubes directly into the tank because they can contain impurities. As a kid, I kept my aquariums warm during winter power failures with a candle inside a tin can. I sunk it halfway into the tank and secured it to the corners with duct tape. The tin would heat up from the flame and raise the water temperature a few degrees. But this is not a long-term solution.

When I was ten, I was fascinated by discus after reading about them in *National Geographic*. At that time, they were rare and difficult to keep. I finally acquired a pair, and once they acclimated, they spawned. When the spawn were two days old, we had a mammoth ice storm and our power went out for seven days in February. I ended up losing the parents and all of the babies. There was nothing I could do to keep those fish alive for a week with no electricity.

Is it a bad idea to place aquariums near air conditioners, heaters, and windows?

Extreme fluctuations in temperature, particularly drops in temperature, can be a problem for fish. Very often in the winter, a cold blast of air from a door left open can drop the temperature in a fish tank 10 or 15 degrees. This stresses the fish and allows dormant ich parasites to flare up on the fish. Rapid rises in temperature cause a decrease in oxygen in the tank. This will kill not only the fish but also the ammonia- and nitrite-consuming bacteria in the tank. These bacteria are aerobic—they need oxygen to survive, so a rapid rise in temperature will compromise your bacteria bed. The resulting rise in ammonia levels can also kill the fish.

Random events are a part of life, and there are situations in which rapid temperature fluctuations are beyond your control. However, putting your aquarium in front of a heater or window where this is bound to happen is simply thumbing your nose at King Neptune, who loves to press Ctrl + Alt + Del on his undersea computer, causing the death of all your fish whenever you take your success as an aquarist for granted.

What do you do to maintain water quality when the electricity goes out?

Battery-operated air pumps work well in a pinch to keep the water aerated. For emergencies, you should also have some air-operated internal filters. Years ago, we used these in all of our aquariums, and they did a fine job. In an emergency, take some of the filter media out of the filters on your tanks that are not working. Put it in the internal box filters. Hook them up to the battery-powered air pump and put this inside the tank. The old filter media will have water from the fish tank flowing through because of the power of the air bubbles and will maintain normal ammonia and nitrite levels in the tank. Your fish may not even notice a power outage.

Of course, if you have several home aquariums, you should keep a generator on hand for emergencies. At our store, we have generators, so I don't need to worry about this. During the frequent power outages on Long Island, frantic aquarists will bring their fish into my store. I cheerfully keep them in a spare tank until the power goes back on.

How much lighting is too much?

Fish do sleep, as any aquarist knows. When you turn on the lights in the morning, you will always find your fish on the bottom of the tank hidden behind rocks. Their colors are pale, and some fish, such as the saltwater parrotfish, actually spin a cocoon of mucus when they are asleep. No scientific studies have been conducted to determine whether continuous light is detrimental to fish. But fish do adapt well to variable periods of light. A pond in Maine may get sixteen hours of daylight in summer and five hours in winter, but the fish in there do just fine.

I have seen fish that were exposed to constant light mainly because the tanks were in children's rooms and the fish lights were used as night-lights. I'm sure that if the fish really needed to sleep, they would do so despite the light, just like any other creature.

A Time-Share for Your Fish

When the weather is nice and we spend a lot of time outside, we also want our pets to spend time outside. It's easy to let our dogs, cats, and rabbits come out with us, but what about our fish? Garden ponds are big these days. The technology to create a large garden pond and keep it filtered and clear is readily available. With a little determination and muscle power, you can dig a hole; line it with plastic; put in a couple of drains, a strong filter, and an ultraviolet light sterilizer; add a waterfall; and—bingo—you have your very own pond.

Bear in mind, however, that these ponds are mainly suitable for goldfish and koi. That is fine with me because I like goldfish and koi very much. They are extremely friendly fish that can be trained to do a lot of things. For instance, I've taught the goldfish in my backyard pond to ring a bell for food. To set up this trick, I first dropped into the pond a fishing sinker attached to a string, which was in turn attached to a bell on land. Then I stood in front of the pond with a handful of food. The fish splashed around the surface, begging for food, but I wouldn't drop any in until a fish hit the fishing sinker. In the beginning, the fish hit the sinker quite by accident. But any time a fish hit it, I threw in some food. In no time at all, they figured out that splashing around the surface didn't make the food come, but hitting the fishing sinker did. At first, I kept the sinker close to the surface so that it was easier for the fish to come in contact with it. Then I began dropping the sinker lower and lower into the pond. The fish would swim down, hit the sinker (which would make the bell ring), and then shoot to the surface to be fed. Of course, the fish made no connection with the bell because they couldn't hear it. All they knew was that when they hit the sinker, food fell in the pond. But my guests sure got a kick out of seeing the fish ring the bell for food.

In the summertime, freshwater tropical fish can also live outside. Most garden centers now sell half-barrel-type garden ponds to put on your patio. If you fill it with water and plant it heavily with oxygenating plants, such as elodea and red papyrus, and a small water lily, this little pond can be quite attractive. You can put some of your aquarium fish in such ponds for the summer. The average well-planted half-barrel pond with a handful of community tropical fish really doesn't even need a filter. The fish will live and spawn in there, and by the end of the summer, you will have some really nice-looking fish for your aquarium as well as lots of babies that you may be able to trade for food and supplies at your local pet store.

If you do want to add a filter to the pond, garden centers sell small mechanical filters combined with ultraviolet light sterilizers. They will keep the water in these little half barrels totally clear. In the past, I have enjoyed letting the ponds become green with algae and adding the fish in late May, not knowing what I would find when I drained the ponds in the fall. The live bearers did amazingly well. The guppies I bred in these half barrels are bigger and better than anything you can buy over the Internet.

Fish also enjoy a summer vacation, and a half-barrel pond can be the perfect way to share the experience with them.

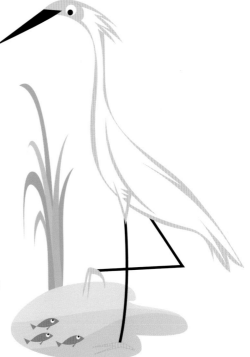

I want to start a backyard pond, but I live near the beach, where there are a lot of birds (such as pelicans and egrets) that prey on fish. How can I keep my fish safe while still having a beautiful pond?

The easiest way to protect fish from predatory birds is to make sure that the edge of the pond is as deep as the middle. Predatory birds like to wade in shallow water to snatch fish. This will be nearly impossible for any egret if the pond is at least 2 feet deep at the edges. Deeper water also makes it easier for the fish to dart out of the way. Unfortunately, species such as goldfish and koi expect to be fed whenever they see any upright being at the water's edge, and some smart egrets have even learned to place bits of bread in the water to attract fish for easy grabbing. The birds will still be able to snatch a few fish from deep water (invariably the most colorful and expensive ones).

To prevent egrets from strolling up to your pond, place 8- to 12-inch-high stakes around the perimeter and string heavy fishing line between them. When the egret approaches, the fishing line will hit the bird's legs, which will usually scare it off. However, a really hungry egret will sometimes perch on these monofilament lines and hunch over the pond, waiting for the fish. In cases like this, the best remedy is an electronic garden protector. This is a thin wire that you thread around the pond through little plastic stakes. A little transformer powered by a 9-volt battery is attached to the wire. Any animal that touches it will get a mild shock.

This system also works to keep raccoons out of the pond. Even if the water at the edge is too deep for raccoons to grab any fish, they will still try. And they can do a lot of damage by knocking rocks into the water, squashing plants, and making a general mess. For most nocturnal predators, the electric fences work very well and can be unplugged during the day.

I built a fish pond and stocked it with goldfish and water lilies and other plants. But the filters recommended by the garden center cost ten times more than the pond itself. Why?

The problem is that our expectations for artificial fish ponds are much higher than they would be for natural ponds. A natural fish pond is hazy. You can barely see the bottom except for those times of the year when algae growth is diminished.

You are aware of the amount of work needed to keep a living room fish tank clear. Imagine taking the fish tank from your living room, putting it in your backyard in full sunlight, and throwing in a few shovels

of dirt for good measure. The filter hanging on that tank would never be able to keep that water clear. Even though you may not deliberately throw shovels of dirt in your fish pond, flowerpots of water lilies and the normal dust and debris in any outdoor environment soon bring about the same effect.

Keeping fish ponds clear is costly. Think of a garden fish pond as a 1,000-gallon aquarium. Just imagine what it will require to keep all of that water clear outdoors, in full sunlight. You will need a bottom drain, a surface skimmer, a high-pressure filter full of beads, and a very strong ultraviolet light sterilizer. Even then, you will need to backwash the beads every few days to flush out accumulating dirt. This type of setup is expensive, but it will ensure clear water in a fish pond. And for most people, there is no point in having a fish pond if they can't see the fish.

Ponds that are heavily planted usually remain clear enough to see the fish. But the tradeoff is that half of the surface is covered by water lilies, so you still can't see the fish all of the time.

We have a garden pond with beautiful goldfish. We have bought turtles and frogs for the pond, but they are always gone the next day. What can we do to make our pond more appealing for them?

Remember where these turtles and frogs come from. They like to live in shallow ponds full of reeds and rushes, with gradual, sloping sides. No frog or turtle is going to feel comfortable in a plastic or concrete pond that is maybe 3 feet deep in the middle and 2 feet deep at the edge, with straight sides and no muddy shallow areas to hide in. In an inhospitable situation, all living things—humans included—are going to strike out on their own to find a better place. Unfortunately, in this situation, that better place usually doesn't exist for turtles and frogs. They have no idea that no other ponds will be found for miles. Most of them end up getting chewed up by your neighbor's lawnmower.

Fish ponds are just that—ponds for fish. If you want turtles and frogs, you should set up a pond strictly for them. Very often, small frogs that grew from

tadpoles in other ponds will strike out, looking for another habitat. They will then colonize your pond on their own. Oddly, those frogs will stay in the pond because they discovered it. To them, it is the perfect place. They will adapt to the lack of shallow areas.

Can fish and aquatic turtles be kept together in one pond?

I have a pond where I keep aquatic turtles, but I have a fence around it to keep them from leaving. Once they have acclimated to the pond, they seem quite content. But I do have some islands in the middle. They feel much more secure sitting on islands than on the bank. But this pond is set up only for turtles, and I have separate ponds in my yard for fish. If it's hard for me to mix the species, it's probably going to be hard for you, too.

Do floating plants require less light because they are closer to the light source?

As a general rule, most aquatic plants prefer strong light, and floating plants usually grow in lakes and rivers in bright, full sun. We use them in fish ponds to provide shade and discourage algae growth. I have never been a fan of floating plants in aquariums. They cut down the amount of light in the tank. And you can't see the flowers or rosettes from the side. All you really see is a big mass of roots hanging in the tank. They are useful in tanks used for spawning, though, because the roots are a great place for fish to lay their eggs.

If you want to keep them for this purpose, put a bunch of floating plants in a bucket of water in a sunny spot. When your fish are spawning, you can pull out a couple and put them in the tank for the fish to use.

> ### JUST A GLIMPSE
> My father had a backyard fish pond. He refused to spend the money for proper filtration and did not want me spending money on him. He wouldn't even let me get the filters and install them as a gift. I recall standing next to his fish pond one day in July, and it was just a soup of green. As we stood there, looking at this dismal scene, a little flash of gold glinted beneath the surface. My father exclaimed, "Look, there's a fish. I saw one two days ago, too." I can't see the point in having a fish pond if you are lucky to glimpse the fish once every two days.

Fish Doctoring

Commercial aquariums utilize the services of amazingly skilled veterinarians. They can anesthetize fish and perform surgery, force-feed fish that refuse to eat, and perform a range of diagnostics to determine what the problem is. Unfortunately, home aquarists are usually at a loss when their fish become ill. They typically go to a pet store, where they can be confronted with a mind-boggling array of remedies that promise to cure every fish ailment imaginable.

Fish are generally prone to these four illnesses:

1. Parasitic infections
2. Bacterial infections
3. Viral infections
4. Adverse reactions to poor water quality

The first step is to determine the problem through process of elimination. If your fish don't look good, start by checking the water. Is the pH too low? Is the ammonia too high?

Sometimes adjusting the pH, doing a water change, or adding additional filtration will resolve the problem. When fish live in poor-quality water, it also compromises their immunity, making them more prone to other infections.

The most common parasitic infection is ich. Its life cycle has been exhaustively studied. Fish can live in a symbiotic relationship with the ich parasite. After all, the parasite needs the fish to survive. If the fish dies, the parasite goes with it. When the fish's metabolism becomes compromised, the parasite starts taking over. The fish finally dies when it becomes infected with a greater number of parasites than it has evolved to tolerate.

Bacterial infections are somewhat harder to treat because you don't know exactly what you are treating without doing cultures and sensitivity tests. Normally, you go into the pet store and the guy in there gives you something to try. Sometimes it works, sometimes not. At the same time, antibiotics that you put in the tank will also kill off the bacteria bed. I've found that it is better to administer antibiotics to fish in their food. This is assuming that the infected fish is still eating. If it is eating dried flakes or pellets, it is fairly easy to crush the antibiotics into a powder and sprinkle it on the pellets or flakes. When feeding these to the fish, first put in a tiny bit of food without medication. The fish will gobble this up, then slowly feed them the medicated food little by little. Today, foods are also made with added medications for parasites or bacterial infections. These work much better than medicating the entire tank. The fish also gets a much more useful dose of medication if it is swallowed rather than absorbed through osmosis. However, this is an inexact science, and much of the available information on this subject is anecdotal. Even my information is based only on my many years of experience; I am not a scientist or a veterinarian.

How do I recognize ich, and what should I do about it?

Ich usually appears as fine spots of salt on the fish, but they are not always visible to the naked eye. The fact that a fish does not have visible white spots is no guarantee that ich is not present. If you notice a fish persistently rubbing against a rock or an ornament in the tank, it may be trying to scrape off ich parasites. The parasite will not go away unless you put a concentration of poison in the tank. It should be strong enough to kill the ich without harming the fish. The poison of choice is copper. Most copper solutions sold in pet shops instruct you to use a much higher dose than necessary. This is dangerous because it's only human nature to think that if one drop is good, two will be better. For instance, a package of copper used to treat saltwater ich recommends a mixture of 0.15 parts per million. During my apprenticeship with Pete Ponziato of the New York Aquarium, I was told that a mixture of 0.05 parts per million was equally effective for killing ich parasites. It was also less likely to compromise the fish or the bacteria bed in the tank. He told me that my aquariums should always have a copper level of 0.05 parts per million if I regularly added new fish that may have had contact with ich parasites. It's better to be proactive than reactive. If you have a fish-only tank, you can keep a low level of copper in the water and use an ultraviolet light sterilizer to keep it free from parasites. Be aware, however, that certain species of fish, including

cories, loaches, and some "scaleless fish, " such as elephantnoses, can be harmed by copper. Do your research beforehand.

Ich causes great problems in saltwater reef tanks. You may see reef tanks full of fish in public aquariums, but these habitats are monitored by professionals twenty-four hours a day. Ich is an invertebrate. A tank with anemones, corals, and shrimp to which you add some fish is a tank full of parasites that can hurt the fish. When adding fish to a reef tank, stick to small, hardy fish such as blennys and clownfish. They will have a better chance of surviving in a tank infested with ich parasites compared to fish like butterflies, angelfish, or tangs. If a fish is strong and healthy, the parasites should not bother it too much. But if you put a newly caught, stressed-out imperator angelfish into a reef tank full of live rock and other organisms, it is sure to be attacked. In its compromised condition, it will suffer. You can put it in a tank with copper solution to kill the ich, but it will be reinfected when you put it back into the reef tank. Choose the fish for your reef tank carefully because some do better than others in symbiotic relationships with parasites.

It also helps to raise the temperature in the aquarium to speed up the life cycle of the ich parasite. When it matures, it leaves the fish. A freshwater fish can also be taken out of the tank and put in a saltwater bath of the same pH and temperature for a very short time. This change in osmotic pressure won't kill the fish, but it will kill the parasites on the fish. Saltwater fish can be placed in a freshwater bath for this treatment. However, this won't help if you put the fish back in a tank that is infested with the ich parasite. You must also have copper in the water of the tank to kill the parasites, and this takes longer than most people realize.

Fresh carbon will remove copper and other medications from an aquarium as fast as they are put in. If the carbon has been in the tank for a couple of weeks, its absorption power is much diminished, and it won't affect the medication in the tank.

Does ich spread easily? How about from one tank to another? Can you cross-contaminate tanks with ich by using the same bucket to change water?

The parasite that we call ich is extremely invasive and durable. In its free-swimming stage, it is easily transferred from one tank to another via fishnets.

This is why good pet stores keep their nets in a bath to sterilize them after each use. Ich is a parasite, and parasites really don't want to kill their hosts. Every animal has a different level of tolerance for parasites, and a healthy fish can easily live with ich parasites on it. These usually are not even visible. However, if the fish is compromised from stress, poor water conditions, or poor diet, the ich parasite will start the fish on a downward spiral. The ich parasite becomes the straw that breaks the camel's back, and the fish will start to die. In a situation like this, in which a fish has many more ich parasites than it would host in nature, that aquarium will also have many more free-swimming parasites that can cross-contaminate.

What is whirling disease, and how do you treat it?

This is a parasite that lives in the fish's nervous system, causing it to twirl. Various forms of it affect different fish. It is even found in stocks of native North American trout. Unfortunately, even our best government ichthyologists have not been able to find a cure. I personally have never seen a fish cured of whirling disease. If a fish in your tank shows symptoms, remove it immediately. However, this is a very uncommon disease in pet fish, so don't worry about it.

Can fish in an already established tank die of stress from adding new fish?

The fish in the tank are not going to be stressed by the addition of new fish, assuming that you are not adding piranhas to a tank full of guppies. However, the bacteria bed in an established aquarium is adjusted to the particular number of fish in the tank at that time. Plus, in many older established tanks, the pH level of the water has dropped considerably as a

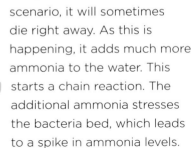

result of undissolved organic matter that has accumulated. The fish in that tank are acclimated to that level and live there quite happily. When you add a new fish to that scenario, it will sometimes die right away. As this is happening, it adds much more ammonia to the water. This starts a chain reaction. The additional ammonia stresses the bacteria bed, which leads to a spike in ammonia levels. This stresses the other fish in the tank and may cause them to die.

So it's really not the addition of a new fish that causes the problems; it's the resulting change in the enclosed environment.

My fish recently got beat up by another fish. Its fins are all torn, and it is hiding up in the corner of the tank. What should I do?

Fish have amazing regenerative powers. However, once a fish becomes targeted, it is doomed unless you separate it from the aggressor. In nature, the losing fish can swim away. In an aquarium, it is trapped. Removing the attacker doesn't always help because the second in command often takes over the bullying. If you have no other way to separate the attacker and its victim, get a maternity tank at a pet store. This can be hooked to the inside of the tank and used to protect the injured fish until it recovers. This is really all you can do to help the fish heal. If it is so badly injured that it refuses to eat, there isn't anything you can do to bring it back. However, if the fish is still eating and you put it into a stress-free situation, the fins and scales will regrow almost like magic. When it is totally healed, don't return it to the tank until you put the dominant fish into your isolation tank.

After a few days, the injured fish will settle in. Then you can let the dominant fish out of the enclosure

FLOATERS OR SINKERS?

Some dead fish float; others sink to the bottom of the tank. It all depends on the amount of gas in the fish when it dies. Most fish have an air bladder that helps them maintain buoyancy in the water. If the air bladder happens to empty out when a fish is dying, it will sink. If the air bladder is full of air when the fish dies, it will float.

and hope that all will be well. But it's up to you as a fish keeper to watch them and make sure that everyone gets along.

What's the best size for a quarantine tank? Is it necessary to go any larger than 10 gallons?

Quarantine tanks are actually a very good idea. The problem is that you can't just set up a quarantine tank with a brand-new filter and put a fish in there. You will have a big spike in nitrite and ammonia levels because the tank has not been cycled.

If you plan to make a quarantine tank for new fish, begin by keeping a small whisper filter hooked onto the back of your established tank. Run it constantly so that it is completely cycled and full of the bacteria needed to reduce ammonia and nitrite levels. When you're almost ready to bring home that new fish, purchase a 10-gallon tank and fill it with fresh or salt water. Take that whisper filter off the back of your established tank and put it onto the 10-gallon quarantine tank. This way, you have a cycled, aged filter and the aerobic bacteria living in the cartridge will consume the ammonia produced by the new fish. Keep the new fish quarantined for a couple of weeks. When the quarantine period is over, throw away the old cartridge, wash and sterilize the filter, put in a new cartridge, and stick it back onto the established aquarium to cycle again so that you will have it ready for any future fish that need to be quarantined.

How do I acclimate a new fish to my aquarium when I bring it home from the pet store?

Usually, the best approach is the drip method. Pour the new fish and the water into a small bucket or Tupperware container and place it on the floor beneath your aquarium. Get some plastic tubing and place one end in the tank and the other end in the bucket. Start a siphon from the aquarium into the bucket. After it starts, tie a knot in the hose so the water drips slowly into the bucket. When the amount of water in the bucket has doubled, the fish can be considered acclimated to the water in your tank. Catch it with a net, put it into your tank, and discard the water in the bucket. Never pour this water into your

Fish in a Bag

When I was a kid, the idea of dripping fish was pretty unknown. Instead, we used to take the bag from the pet store and float it in our aquarium. When the temperature equalized, we cut open the bag and let the fish swim into the tank. This usually worked, and I still use this method when the fish in the bag is obviously distressed and time is short. But it is not ideal because you don't know what is in the water you're releasing into your tank. When you arrive home from the pet store with your fish in that little bag, it has been breathing very quickly and urinating in that water. Consequently, the ammonia level has increased and the pH level of that water has dropped. Dumping 2 cups of that liquid into your tank won't really alter the chemistry. But if you dump six bags of fish into the tank, that may add 12 cups of low-pH water with high concentrations of ammonia, and that will definitely change the chemistry of your tank.

tank. It may contain parasites or diseases from the pet store. Of course, the fish could also transmit these problems. But a water change never hurts.

What other factors need to be considered when you are deciding how to acclimate a new fish to an aquarium?

When we get a very expensive saltwater fish from overseas here in our store, we first test the pH and temperature of the water the fish came with. In most cases, it's cold, very acidic, and very high in ammonia. Ammonia will not be that harmful to fish if the pH is low. If we used the drip method, the pH would rise and the high ammonia level would start to compromise the fish. So instead we prepare a solution of new water and lower its temperature and pH to match the water in the bag. Next, we gently move the fish from the bag into this acclimation tank. Then we start the dripping process into the acclimation tank. This way, the fish acclimates to our water in a solution containing no ammonia at all.

However, there have been extreme situations when this complicated process wasn't possible. If the fish is dying on arrival, we take it out of the bag, throw it in a tank, and hope for the best. We have a fairly good success rate doing it that way.

We once imported a baby black tip reef shark (not for most aquarists!) from Indonesia to put in a custom-made oval 1,000-gallon tank for a customer. The airline made a mistake, and this shark went around the world twice before landing at John F. Kennedy International Airport, in New York. We rushed the box to the store, opened it, and gazed into the black lagoon. Somewhere in that disgusting mess was a baby black tip reef shark, most likely dead. I reached into the murky mess to find the baby shark, pulled it out, and gazed at it despondently. The fish twitched, and I realized it was still alive. I threw it into a 500-gallon tank and watched it sink to the bottom, where it lay immobile on its back. At first the situation didn't look too promising, but the shark suddenly started to breathe again. I put my hand in the tank and kept swishing the shark back and forth so the water would flush through its gills until it gradually began to recover and swim on its own. When acclimating a big shark at public aquariums, they actually walk them back and forth in the water to accomplish the same thing. The shark stayed on its back for twenty-four hours and then gradually started to come around. By the next day, the baby shark was eating. It lived in that customer's tank for seven years until it became too large and was donated to a public aquarium. (It is better, however, not to get any fish that will outgrow its tank; not all aquariums will take them.)

Everybody's an Expert

I've kept fish with my good friend Russell Taylor since grammar school. He currently breeds show-quality ranchu goldfish and is an active member of the American Goldfish Society. He told me that members of the American Goldfish Society wrote to the Children's Television Workshop regarding the Muppet character Elmo. On the show *Sesame Street*, Elmo kept a pet goldfish, Dorothy, in a little bowl. As we know, it is inhumane to keep goldfish in bowls, and members of the goldfish society thought this set a bad example for children. But the comments fell of deaf ears, and Dorothy stayed in the bowl.

One day, my long-suffering producer from *The Martha Stewart Show,* Jocelyn Santos, told me that Martha's production company had struck a deal with the owners of the Muppets, and I would be doing some segments with Muppets. I really wanted to do a segment with Big Bird, but he was too tall to fit in our studio. When I learned that I would be doing a segment with Elmo instead, I saw it as the perfect opportunity

to spring Dorothy from her fishbowl. I devised a segment in which Elmo and I decided that Dorothy shouldn't be in the fishbowl, and we proceeded to put together a large 20-gallon aquarium and put Dorothy in the tank with some new goldfish companions.

For comic relief, I brought my scarlet macaw, Harry, and my African Grey parrot, Darwin. The segment went beautifully. Elmo and I went through all of the steps of putting the tank together: adding the filter, gravel, and water and taking out the chlorine. Elmo was very cute and happy, and Harry bit him on the nose right on cue. Darwin broke the rubber bands on the plastic bags holding the fish before we put them into the tanks. At the end of the segment, Elmo looked into Dorothy's fishbowl and commented that it looked so sad and empty. I fixed that by putting a betta into the bowl and explained that, when properly cared for, this type of fish can thrive in a fishbowl.

The episode aired a few weeks later, and soon afterward the producers gave me a big stack of letters divided into three groups. Some were from goldfish fanatics complaining that the tank I set up was too small and I added too many fish too quickly, which was bound to give children a bad impression. The second stack of letters came from people who objected to my statement that keeping goldfish in bowls was inhumane. All of these people had kept their goldfish happily in bowls for nine or ten years. One woman actually said that her goldfish had lived in a bowl for nine years; she carried goldfish and bowl from room to room to ensure that her fish didn't get lonely. I also received many letters from betta lovers who objected to my putting a betta into Dorothy's empty fishbowl. They felt that this implied that bettas were more disposable than goldfish.

When I showed those letters to my friend Russell, he was embarrassed because a lot of them came from people he knew in his goldfish club. He had helped me put the script together for the segment and fully expected that the gold-fish society members would be pleased that we got Dorothy liberated from her bowl on national television. He had no idea that his club members had "so much time on their hands" and did not have a better understanding of the intent of that segment, which was basically that tanks are good and bowls are bad for goldfish. I was truly amazed that so many people would overreact to advice presented by me, a puppet, and two parrots. That episode has since gone into syndication, and it pops up all over the world. Every time it does, I get a similar assortment of letters. I don't let it bother me because I learned long ago that you can't make everyone happy no matter how hard you try.

What is the absolutely most aggressive aquarium fish that can be bought in a store?

Well, piranhas cannot be legally sold in most states, so that tells you something. Snakeheads cannot be sold in any state, which should also tell you something. African tigerfish are aggressive, and lionfish can be aggressive. Some groupers can be aggressive, but all of these fish can be legally sold in every state.

However, the term *aggressive* is rather subjective. Highly carnivorous fish will eat other fish, but technically that's not aggression. It's hunger. Some fish are extremely territorial and will chase other fish entering their territory, but defending territory is not the same as aggression. Problems occur when a fish with a strong food drive is placed in a tank with other fish that it considers to be food. It will not stop until it has consumed them. To us, this looks aggressive.

Likewise, if a fish with strong territorial behavior starts defending its territory from a fish that cannot escape from the territory, it won't stop until that fish is dead. This doesn't fit my definition of aggression either.

The most territorially defensive fish I ever owned was a big red devil named Herman, who thought the entire world was his to defend. He lived alone in a 90-gallon tank in our living room, having killed all of the other fish in his tank. Not only did Herman consider other fish as intruders that needed to be disposed of, but he also thought that algae cleaning sticks needed to be chased away. Even the rocks in his tank bothered him—he kept moving them around. He also viewed humans and dogs the same way. Whenever someone entered the living room, Herman rushed to the glass and tried to chase him away.

What is the best time to introduce new fish to a tank to keep aggression down (at night, after feeding, before feeding)?

This is always a touchy situation, and I have not figured out a foolproof solution yet. It seems sensible to introduce a new fish at night. If you turn off the lights, the other fish won't have a chance to beat it up right away. But many times I have done this only to discover, when I turned on the lights in the morning, that the new fish was up in the corner of the tank with its fins in tatters.

Another method is to remove all rocks and decorations, stir the gravel until it is cloudy, and reposition everything. The fish may not notice a new addition to the tank in the resulting confusion. But this doesn't always work either, and it may affect the pH level in your tank. Stirring up the tank will also dislodge any undesirable organic material that may be buried in the gravel bed. Organic matter can create pockets of hydrogen sulfide gas. When the water is disturbed, these will be released and may potentially affect the pH level.

I have had the most success with an isolation tank used for live-bearing fish. This is basically a little mesh cage that hangs in the aquarium. Place the two most dominant fish in the isolation tank for a few days to prevent them from attacking the new fish. Very often, if you remove only the most dominant fish, the second in command will take over beating up the new fish. There is no point in putting the dominant fish in a separate tank. They will have no opportunity to learn about the new fish, and you will face the same situation as soon as you put them back together. The isolation tank lets them get used to each other's smell and look. When you return the dominant fish to the general population, the tank is less likely to turn into a battlefield. This works particularly well with African cichlids.

There are no hard and fast rules about how to prevent problems. Every situation is different and requires a unique approach. In a pinch, I have used a Tupperware container punched full of holes to isolate an aggressive fish. Sink the container with the fish inside to the bottom of the tank and leave it there for a day or two. This fish lockdown has worked well to cool off a fish's aggressive tendencies. Sometimes a fish keeper must think like the warden of an aggressive prison population and do whatever works when a riot is raging.

Of a large batch of hundreds of fry, how many will typically live if the conditions are good?

If the conditions are ideal, every one that isn't suffering from a genetic abnormality could survive. But conditions are rarely ideal. And you really wouldn't want any defective fry to survive, because you would inevitably have to cull them out as they got bigger.

Technically, no one can predict the percentage of fry that will be defective. The genetic health of the spawn depends on the genetic health of the parents. If either parent carries lethal genes, fewer fry will survive.

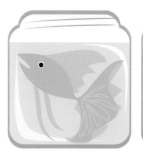

When I was a kid, I must have had two hundred fry the first time I spawned bettas. These became free-swimming after the male parent abandoned the bubble nest. I had baby-food jars all over the house, each containing one tiny betta. Fortunately, it was summer and the house was warm, so it wasn't a problem keeping them at the proper temperature to promote growth. There was a kettle pond near my house with lots of daphnia colonies. After a month of this intensive labor, I found that many of the baby bettas had crooked spines, short fins, or other abnormalities. So I ended up giving them to my oscars.

I bought a pair of swordtails, a pair of platys, and a pair of guppies from my local pet store. What do I do if they have babies?

Breeding fish has been my hobby since I was five. Live-bearing fish are the easiest to breed. The most popular are guppies, platys, swordtails, and mollies. Quite a few others have live babies, but they are more difficult to raise. Actually, in this day and age, mollies are no longer that easy to keep either. When we were kids, we always bought breeding traps because we were afraid that the adult fish would eat the newborn fry. In reality, baby fish are not truly born. The mother fish doesn't provide any nourishment to the babies; she just keeps the eggs inside of her until they hatch and the babies develop. Then, the babies are released. *Live-bearing* is really a misnomer. They should be called "fish that retain their eggs until they hatch internally," but that's a little long.

The breeding trap was a plastic box with holes. The female was put in the top part. There was a little v-shaped opening to the bottom compartment.

When the babies were born, they fell through opening into the bottom compartment where the mother could not get to them. When they were all born, we removed them to another tank and they did fine. However, I eventually had so many fish that it became hard to keep track of who was pregnant and move them to the breeding traps. I noticed that in the tanks that contained only live-bearing fish, the adults never even tried to eat the babies. They coexisted happily. This was only a problem in community tanks that contained tiger barbs or angelfish that normally didn't share the same habitat as the live-bearing fish. Angelfish were particularly fond of eating baby guppies and swordtails, much to my horror.

Once I made this discovery, I dispensed with breeding traps in my tanks of live-bearing fish. They seemed unnecessary. Of course, the size of my tanks had something to do with the decision too. It can be hard for newly born fry to maneuver in a large 20- or 30-gallon tank. The current is too strong, and it is hard for them to find food. In this situation, the fry would probably be more comfortable in a breeding trap until they are about half an inch long. Then you can put them back with the parent fish unless the tank contains fin nippers or carnivorous fish. In that case, it is better to keep the babies in the breeding trap as long as possible.

Why do the guppies in my tank have babies all the time but my goldfish never do?

A guppy is full grown when it is an inch long. But the goldfish that we win at carnivals are not mature until they are 8 or 9 inches long. They don't start breeding until they reach 6 or 7 inches, and this doesn't often happen in a home aquarium. If kept in optimal conditions, a goldfish can reach breeding age in a year. However, very few aquariums are optimal for this. The best goldfish breeders keep them in extremely large tanks or outdoor ponds to encourage maximum growth and show potential.

It's also hard to tell male and female goldfish apart. When the males are in breeding condition, they develop hard bumps on their gill plates. They use these to rub against the females sides and stimulate egg laying. These bumps disappear when breeding season ends, and males and females become virtually indistinguishable. These issues account for the rarity of impromptu goldfish breeding in home aquariums.

Lessons from the Fish

My parents gave me my first 10-gallon aquarium as a Christmas gift when I was five. The fish in that tank were a pair of swordtails, a pair of angelfish, two kissing gouramis, a catfish, and two guppies. The guppies promptly had babies. Since the man in the pet store warned me that the angelfish would eat the babies, I put the babies in a glass jar and took them to my kindergarten classroom. The teacher, Mrs. Graypeck, a very nice lady, made a big deal over the fish, and we set up a little aquarium in the class. She paid for the tank, the filter, and everything else herself. We enjoyed watching the babies grow up and have babies of their own during the school year. When school ended in June, Mrs. Graypeck distributed the guppies among the children who were interested in keeping them. She took the tank down, planning to set it up again the following September.

That fall, my parents put me in Catholic school. The sister had a much different, stricter philosophy about education, and the classroom was not a happy place. Recalling the joy that the guppies had brought to my kindergarten class, I decided to take some to my first-grade class, hoping it would soften up the sister and bring pleasure to my classmates. Proudly, I arrived with my glass jar full of guppies and asked her if we could keep them in our classroom. Her response was to take me to the boys' restroom and force me to pour the guppies into the toilet and flush them away. "School," she told me sternly, "is for learning, nothing more."

I will say this for the sister: the somber, intimidating tone in her classroom motivated us to successfully learn our academic lessons, and I was able to skip ahead academically the next year. But the sister herself failed to learn an essential lesson—that caring for animals can teach children (and adults) to be better, more responsible, more compassionate people.

I am fascinated by the way my African cichlids pick up their babies in their mouths and carry them around. But I can't help wondering what prevents these parent fish from eating their babies.

This answer is not quite so cut-and-dried. According to scientists, when fish are in breeding condition, their hormones inhibit their desire to eat. This may be the case for fish that brood in their mouths exclusively. But I personally think there is a bit more to it. I clearly remember watching one of my male cichlids picking up babies one by one and carrying them back to the nest. These were not mouth brooders, and they did eat while caring for their babies. I put some frozen bloodworms in the tank just as this father was gathering up his stray babies. He had one in his mouth as a bloodworm floated down in front of him. He quickly snatched it and then just hovered in the water. Suddenly he spit out both the baby and the bloodworm, ate the bloodworm, picked up the baby and continued carrying it to the nest. This reaction wasn't due to hormones or instinct. This fish displayed some kind of cognitive decision-making process. That fish remained stationary for a minute, deciding what to do. I have told this story to many ichthyologists, but none have ever stated definitively whether this was a demonstration of cognitive ability or some kind of instinct that kicked in. Most likely it was instinct, because evolution would dictate that a fish could respond this way in this type of situation. But I still like to think of it as an example of fish cognition, because I happen to like fish more than most scientists.

Is it always true that clear eggs are fertile and brown eggs are infertile?

It depends on which type of fish laid the eggs. The only universal rule is that white eggs are always infertile or dead. White eggs will develop fungus right away. So this is the most important thing to look for. Fertile eggs can be clear, brown, or black, but white fuzzy eggs are never going to hatch.

When suckerfish cling to the glass, how do they make suction and also breathe? Do they breathe through another organ?

An algae eater doesn't actually hang onto the glass of an aquarium via suction. The lips of the fish have very fine grasping teeth, which it uses to grab the side of the tank, which is not as smooth as you think it is. If you watch carefully, you can see that the fish is able to open and close its mouth, and water flows through its gills and out of the corners of its mouth as it does with any

FISH TRAVEL IN EARLIER DAYS

Fish have been successfully moved all over the world. Before air travel was commonplace, fish were moved from one country to another in metal containers with tight-fitting lids and frequent water changes. Back in the 1950s, a fish importer had tanks built into a cargo ship to import fish from Indonesia. Those tanks had air pumps hooked up to the ship's generators, and the fish lived there quite happily. But you don't need anything quite so elaborate to move your fish if you are driving to your new home.

other fish. The suckerfish's use of its grasping teeth is comparable to a gecko's use of the grasping pads on its toes to hold onto the side of a terrarium.

I was reading the dos and don'ts of fish keeping—on FishChannel—and they said not to flush fish down the toilet. Why? What's wrong with it?

First, if it's a live fish, it's certainly an issue of cruelty. Imagine what a live fish goes through when you do that. Second, if you live in an area where the wastewater goes into sewers, it is possible for pathogens from aquarium fish (live or dead) to be transmitted to native fish populations. Even though the water enters a treatment plant where raw sewage is filtered out, the chemists don't routinely test the water for fish pathogens before it enters our oceans and rivers. This can introduce new diseases into native fish populations.

Aquarists must be responsible and balance their hobbies with the welfare of native wildlife. Many fish and game laws come about because irresponsible fish keepers directly or indirectly introduce nonnative fish or pathogens into our precious North American water system. There is always a better choice for disposing of a fish you don't want than flushing it down the toilet or turning it loose in a pond. Put it in a bucket, take it to your local fish store, and ask the store manager to find a nice home for it. People do this to me all the time. As long as you don't expect any payment or a trade, almost every fish store will happily take your unwanted fish off your hands.

My two-year-old has an aquarium in his room, and I leave the light on as a nightlight, from about 8 p.m. to 7 a.m. During the day, the light is off and the room stays dark with the curtains closed. The fish seem unbothered—in fact, they are thriving. Any thoughts about this?

You answered the question yourself—the fish are thriving. I am assuming that since this fish tank is in a child's bedroom, it contains either goldfish or freshwater community fish such as tetras or barbs. In that situation, you need not worry about available light. Freshwater fish are adaptable. Just think of what happens outdoors. They may experience a week of cloudy weather and rain, then it gets sunny for a week, and the fish do fine either way. Evolution has adapted fish to tolerate changes in available light. I have not seen light have a significant effect on the overall health of freshwater fish.

Marine fish, however, are different. They are in bright sunlight most of the time. Storms come and go across the ocean, but they never result in a week or ten days of dark cloudy weather as happens in inland situations. Saltwater fish really do need light, and the right kind of light, to maintain good color. When kept in captivity with less than optimal light, their colors fade quickly.

How do you do long-distance moves with fish? What equipment do I need for moving my fish and tank?

You will need to purchase a live-bait well with an aerator run on a battery. These are available from sporting-goods companies. Two weeks before the move, get an old-fashioned internal box filter, fill it with floss and carbon, and put it in your established tank running with an air pump. The ammonia-consuming bacteria in your tank will colonize this filter because you have provided an oxygen-rich media bed via the floss and carbon.

Moving the fish tank should be your last chore on moving day. Fill the live-bait well with water from the tank and transfer all of the fish into it. Pull the box filter out of the tank, put it in the live-bait well, and hook it up to the battery-powered air pump. You have now created a temporary cycled tank in which to transport your fish. The bacteria in the box filter will consume most of the ammonia that the fish produce during their stay in the bait well. Unplug the filters in your established tank and drain only enough of the water to move them. Make sure that the media inside of the filters remains wet so that the bacteria in there do not die. If a filter hangs on the back of the tank, you may need to wrap the whole thing in plastic wrap to retain the moisture. Unplug the heaters and let them cool off before you pull them out of the water. Siphon the water from the tank into a sink or out the window. (Out the window is much easier.) Load everything into the moving van.

As soon as you arrive at your new home, set up the tank. Ideally, you should have a new garbage can filled with properly aged water of the proper pH. However, if you don't have an opportunity to arrange this in advance, you will

A CARTON OF FISH
Years ago, fish purchased from pet stores were put into little Chinese-food cartons. The fish didn't always do very well in these because the boxes would start leaking on the way home. Some pet stores preferred to sell their fish in small glass jars. As kids, we would rummage through the neighborhood trash for empty jars. We would wash them out and take them to the pet store to exchange for a few mollies or guppies. The advent of plastic bags revolutionized fish transport.

have to fill your tank with whatever water is available. If it's hose water, it will be about 55 degrees, and you will need to add some hot water to get the temperature right. Test the pH and try to match the level that was previously in your tank. If you fill the tank with raw water, you will have to add a water conditioning product to remove the chlorine and help the fish acclimate.

Put the filters back and plug them in. Some, but not all, of the beneficial bacteria will have died. When everything is running, start acclimating the fish to the water. Use plastic tubing to slowly drip water from the tank into the bait well so that they can gradually get used to the new water. However, if the fish are starting to look distressed in the bait well, you will need to put them right into the tank and take your chances.

THE LUCK OF THE MOVE

I've moved tanks for many of my customers, and, like all aspects of fish keeping, there is a certain element of luck involved. Sometimes I've done everything by the book and all the fish have died. Sometimes I have rushed the fish to their new place in a bucket. They have all been belly up in the bucket but did just fine when placed in their new tank. King Neptune is very fickle when it comes to awarding the good-luck-fish-keeping prize.

How long can a fish last from the time you leave a fish store until you get it home? Is forty-five minutes too long?

If the fish has pure oxygen in the bag, it can theoretically do OK for forty-eight hours. When fish are exported from wholesalers to pet stores, they are packed with pure oxygen and can live this way for several days as long as the temperature is fine. I have had many shipments of fish lost by airlines. When we finally tracked them down three or four days later, we expected the worst. But often we opened the box to find most of the fish still alive because they were packed properly.

Even if no oxygen is used in the bagging process, a fish should last three or four hours if there is enough water in the bag. I cannot imagine any pet store bagging fish in such a way that they would only last forty-five minutes. It's to their advantage for your fish to arrive home hale and hearty.

What are the maximum temperature and pH ranges most fish can safely tolerate in a twenty-four-hour period?

This depends on the fish. Some have evolved in areas of the world where temperatures fluctuate wildly. In its native habitat, the desert pupfish tolerates water that can be 110 degrees during the day and 40 degrees at night. It's much harder for fish to tolerate fluctuations in pH. Even though the water temperature can vary in a native environment, the pH usually remains fairly consistent. However, some fish are hardier than others. A common goldfish or guppy can tolerate much more stress than most fish can. Some, such as bettas, can even tolerate being out of water for short periods as long as their skins remain wet. The best way to determine the answer to this question is to determine the native habitat of the particular fish. If the native regions are subject to extreme ranges in temperature, then that fish should be able to tolerate fluctuations in a home aquarium.

What happens when a saltwater fish is placed in fresh water, and vice versa?

This depends on the fish. Salt water is much denser than fresh water, and saltwater species evolved to tolerate that particular osmotic pressure. When the osmotic pressure suddenly changes, water either rushes into or out of the fish's cell structure, thus compromising it. Some fish, such as trout, salmon, and eels, can swim from salt water into fresh water and vice versa. These fish evolved to tolerate this kind of stress, and their cell structure can adapt to varying osmotic pressure. Other fish, particularly guppies and mollies, which normally live in brackish water, can also do this as long as the transition is gradual. I have kept both of these fish in fresh water and salt water. Still other fish can't tolerate it no matter how gradually it is done, although freshwater fish can tolerate much more salt in the water than we realize. Most saltwater fish can tolerate rapid drops in salinity. But the best way to determine the tolerance level of a particular species is to examine its native habitat. A fish that normally lives in a coral reef at the bottom of the ocean probably has not evolved to be able to adapt to changes in osmotic pressure.

What is the most intelligent fish that can be kept in home aquaria? What can they learn to do (that is, what tricks)?

Most people tend to think of predatory animals as more intelligent than prey species. This is not true of fish or any other animal. Predatory fish such as oscars, lionfish, groupers, and moray eels seem more intelligent than tetras, danios, butterfly fish, and tangs, perhaps because, in nature, predators appear more strategic in seeking out prey. Prey species always live longer if they run from everything. However, once they relax and learn that they have nothing to fear, they demonstrate levels of intelligence equal to those of predatory species. This is obvious to anyone who has trained a rat, a rabbit, or a horse, which can all be taught to perform any behavior that their respective body structures permit. This is equally true of fish. A fish can learn as long as it feels safe. In my opinion, cichlids are the most intelligent freshwater fish, and groupers are the smartest saltwater fish. Any fish that will remain still, observe its surroundings, and base its actions on that information is intelligent. The behavior of some fish species is dictated completely by instinct, but a few of them will tailor their actions to individual situations. I would almost describe it as observational learning.

Any fish will make the association between a person entering the room and the possibility that food is forthcoming. They will rush right to the surface of the tank when they see you coming. Through positive-reinforcement training methods, fish can be taught to do all sorts of things. I previously mentioned that I've taught them to ring bells when they want to be fed by touching a weight suspended in the water that was attached by a string to a bell. They quickly learned to touch the weight and make the bell ring when they wanted food.

FISH U.

Depending on your time and patience, you can train your fish to do many things. Online, you can find videos of goldfish swimming through hoops and performing other tricks. This is a new aspect of pet keeping that many fish keepers are discovering.

If I keep a fish native to my area, would it be illegal or harmful to the fish to release it into the wild?

Whether it is legal or not (often it is not), releasing a fish into the wild is unethical and harmful. Our

waterways and native fish populations are already in serious danger from aquarium fish that have been introduced into these habitats. Anyone who has gone fishing in Florida knows that you catch a lot more oscars, managuenses, and other South American cichlids than largemouth bass. Nonnative species are muscling out the native fish.

Your question was about native fish, so I assume that you have sunfish, crappies, or bass in your aquarium. If you originally caught these fish in a pond, you may think it is OK to return them to the wild. But they may have picked up pathogens through contact with fish that you purchased at a pet store. In a perfect world, you would have a fish pond in your backyard for fish that you no longer want in your aquarium. This prevents any contact with wild fish. It is a fact that introducing aquarium fish into the wild is going to compromise some aspect of the ecological balance and should not be done.

Forgotten Technology

As kids, we were always told how important it was to keep our aquariums free of uneaten food and other organic debris. This was usually accomplished by siphoning the bottom of the tank, but sometimes we didn't have time for that. All pet shops sold a neat little device called a dip tube. It was a long glass or plastic tube with a bulb at the base. Some were more sophisticated, but they all worked the same way. You put your finger on the top of the tube and put it down into the tank near the uneaten food on the bottom. The tube was full of air, which prevented water from rushing in. When you removed your finger and the air left the tube, the water and debris rushed into it. When you put your finger back on the tube, it created a vacuum, allowing you to pull the debris neatly out of the tank. We also used dip tubes when our live-bearing fish had babies. We had to remove them before they were eaten by the adults, and this little tool was perfect for catching each baby without upsetting all of the others by swishing a net around the tank.

It was a great invention, and I used it all the time. But for some reason, manufacturers discontinued this nifty product. Dip tubes went the way of internal filters made with glass wool, stainless steel tanks with slate bottoms, and all of the other obsolete items of aquarium history.

Many years later, I had a meeting with the owners of a company about a sponsorship for their products. They offer many aquarium products, so I suggested that they start making dip tubes again. Everyone in the board room shrugged their shoulders and asked what a dip tube was. I explained it, and they all agreed that it was a good idea. Of course, as in most corporations, no one ever got around to it.

But you can do the same thing with some rigid plastic tubing: cut to the length you want and use it as I described. It may not have the little bulb at the end, but it will still do a good job of removing debris from the bottom of the tank.

I have heard that undergravel filters should not be used with planted tanks. Is this true and, if so, why?

The jury is still out on this. My experience with this has been mixed. There are many other factors that influence the growth of plants in aquariums, including the number of fish in the tank, the amount of natural algae buildup, and the amount of light. I've had very good and very bad experiences growing plants in undergravel filter tanks. I've also had good and bad luck with planted tanks that did not have undergravel filters.

When you do have plants in these tanks, significant root growth can impede the flow of water through the gravel, thus rendering the undergravel filter useless. This arrangement is more likely to compromise the filter than the plants. The whole point of an undergravel filter is to create an even water flow through the gravel bed to provide the maximum amount of well-oxygenated substrate to encourage the growth of ammonia- and nitrite-converting bacteria. A thick growth of plant roots will defeat the purpose.

Some plants, including bunch plants such as cabomba and hornwort, have much less root growth than do Amazon swords and Cryptocorynes. These bunch plants will grow in almost any kind of water, so they are much less likely to cause problems in a tank with an undergravel filter. When planting any type of bunch plant, remember to remove the lead holding the bunch together. Separate the sprigs and push each one into the gravel bed individually.

Whenever I change my canister filter, I can't get it to start again. I fill it with water according to the directions and plug it in, but there is always an air bubble in the line that prevents the water from flowing. What am I doing wrong?

Clean the filter. Do not fill the canister up with water. Put the whole thing back together dry. Then take the outtake hose and breathe on it so that water starts flowing from the tank, up into the intake hose, and down the tube, and starts filling the canister from the bottom. You can feel air being pushed out of the outtake hose. Once the canister is filled, reconnect the outtake hose and plug in the filter; it should work just fine.

Most pet shops sell valves that can be put on the hoses to maintain the water siphon level. Attach these valves to the hoses as close to the canister filter as possible. When it is time to clean the filter, shut off the valve, disconnect the filter from the valve, and clean the filter. The hoses themselves are still filled with water. After the filter is clean, you can fill it with water, put it back down, and reconnect the valves. And you will still have the uninterrupted water flow through the hoses and filter. When you plug in the filter, it should run just fine.

The filter hanging on the back of my aquarium has a cartridge composed of a plastic skeleton that fits inside a little bag of floss. Staff at the pet store advised me not to throw out the plastic skeleton when I change the cartridge. They said I should buy new bags and put the same plastic skeleton inside. Is this good advice?

Quite a bit of beneficial aerobic bacteria grow on the ridges and abrasions on this plastic skeleton. Since they need oxygen to grow, this extremely well-oxygenated plastic skeleton is an ideal environment. When you throw out the old cartridge, all of this useful bacteria goes with it. The bacteria will eventually recolonize the new cartridge, but why throw it away and start all over again if you don't need to? Plus, it is a lot cheaper to simply replace the bags.

The same principle applies when you clean out the internal box filter. There are a lot of bacteria colonizing the floss inside the box filter. Always save some of the old floss and incorporate it with the new floss to jumpstart the bacteria growth.

CANISTER FILTERS

People assume that canister filters sit on the floor and suck the water through the intake hose and push it out of the outtake hose. That's not how it works at all. The water siphons from the tank into the bottom of the canister, flows to the top of the canister, and is pushed out the top of the canister by the impeller. Remember that the water must siphon from the tank into the filter in an uninterrupted flow. The water enters the canister through the bottom and fills the canister to the top so that there are no air bubbles between the tank and the top of the canister.

What is/are the best organism(s) to keep in a sump or a refugium to enhance and provide natural filtration to a saltwater reef tank?

Live plants such as mangrove roots and noninvasive Caulerpa provide the most natural cover. In bays, marshes full of eel grass provide a natural refugium for our oceans, allowing small crustaceans to breed and creating natural filtration through the plant

roots. Passing the tank water through an artificial marsh will accomplish the same thing. Refugium keeping can be as fun and involved as any other type of fish keeping. It is the saltwater aquarist's alternative to a freshwater planted tank.

How long can you have the power off on filters before the nitrifying bacteria start to die? For water changes, I turn everything off as my intakes and heater become exposed. During this time, most of my filter media is not submerged. Is there a certain time frame that I have to get the replacement water back in and power on?

A lot depends on the amount of bacteria in your filters to begin with and the quality of the water it has been living in. Years ago, I used to purchase live bacteria, which were shipped overnight in refrigerated containers and guaranteed to be alive on receipt. I never had much luck with this, but the seller guaranteed that the bacteria could survive twenty-four hours without oxygenated water during shipment. In view of that guarantee, I would imagine that the bacteria could also survive for twelve hours outside of a home aquarium. So I doubt it will be much of an issue for the two or three hours during which you probably have everything turned off to clean your aquarium and do a water change. It has never been an issue for me.

I don't understand how an undergravel filter works. What is reverse flow? What is the difference between using air and powerheads?

I can empathize with your question. These were precisely my thoughts when I first saw an undergravel filter in action. An undergravel filter is a plastic plate across the bottom of the tank with a layer of gravel on top of it. In reality, the gravel never comes in contact with the bottom of the tank. A plastic stem is attached to the plate. Usually a small motor called a powerhead is placed on top of the plastic stem. As air travels up the stem, the water travels along with it. This water comes from under the plate, and, to replace it, water must flow from the tank down through the gravel bed. In this way, water circulates through the tank continuously.

The submersible powerhead causes the water to circulate much, much faster, of course. The more stems you have on the undergravel filter plate, the more water will circulate through the entire gravel bed.

Water continuously flows through the gravel bed and creates a well-oxygenated substrate for bacteria to colonize. This provides the biological filtration. But it doesn't do much to keep your water clear. For that, you need a mechanical filter that will push the water through floss and carbon. So you must have both mechanical and biological filtration for the fish to thrive.

In a reverse-flow undergravel filter, the powerheads push the water down the stemS. The water flows under and back up through the gravel. In theory, the water pushed up through the gravel also pushes organic material up into the tank, where it is removed from the water by the mechanical filter. The theory is good, but the system doesn't always work as well as it should. Much of the debris becomes trapped in the gravel bed, and it is difficult to dislodge. It would take a power washer to push it through.

Do undergravel filters require much maintenance?

Undergravel filters do need maintenance, as they can become clogged. Since water will always take the path of least resistance, it ends up flowing through the gravel bed near the stems of the powerheads. This can be prevented by making the gravel bed deeper near the stems and shallower in the rest of the tank. Large rocks and ornaments can also block the water flow through the gravel bed, thus compromising the biological filtration. You must periodically stir the gravel bed and use a siphon to clean out any debris.

But an undergravel filter is quite a good mechanism, and we used it for many years before the advent of the wet/dry filter.

How does a wet/dry filter work? It seems so complicated to me.

Although it seems complicated, a wet/dry filter operates on the same principle as any other filter does. A wet/dry filter is a glass, acrylic, or plastic box under the aquarium. There is another box suspended inside it that contains some type of plastic media. The box containing the media is separate from the box housing the water that flows in from the tank. Some people assume that water is sucked out of the tank via the hoses in the aquarium, but this isn't how it works. The water actually overflows from the tank into a pipe connecting the tank to the wet/dry filter. The tank water flows down the pipe and then trickles through the media holding the bacteria for biological filtration. Since the media is actually in the air with water flowing through it, it receives an intense amount of oxygen. This is why it is called a wet/dry filter.

Another pump moves the water from the wet/dry filter or sump, and pushes it back into the tank. This is the simplest way to describe the process. Some wet/dry filters can be turned into miniature sewer treatment plants with the addition of protein skimmers, ultraviolet light sterilizers, and denitrification filters. Some people even turn them into refugiums with the addition of various plants. Whatever it takes to keep the water quality high can be placed inside the sump, leaving your aquarium looking pristine, free of hoses, gadgets, and bubbles.

I keep reading about saltwater hobbyists using protein skimmers. What is the point of this? Can I use one in my freshwater aquarium?

Protein skimmers can be tricky, but they serve a great purpose in saltwater aquariums. The best way to describe how a protein skimmer works is to think about how a bubble forms. When you blow a bubble, it floats through the air, gradually losing its viscosity, and finally appears almost dusty before it pops.

In a protein skimmer, water from the tank passes through a plastic column containing a current of very fine bubbles. The bubbles move from the bottom to the top of the column, where they pop. As the bubbles flow through the water, raw waste sticks to them. When a bubble reaches the top of the column and hits the air, it pops. The attached waste products slide out of the water from the explosion of the bubble, and they are contained in a collecting cup to prevent them from reentering the tank. This is filtration in its most basic form. When you look in the collecting cup in a protein skimmer, you will find extremely foul residue. Although protein skimmers are not essential for saltwater tanks, the scum they collect certainly doesn't do the fish any good, so if you can incorporate one into your tank, by all means do so. Be aware, however, that they can be fickle, and it takes a while to get the water column and air column just right. The bubbles must hit at the correct height so that the undissolved elements—proteins—are skimmed off of the water rather than going back in.

Protein skimmers are not used in freshwater systems because fresh water is not dense enough to form fine enough bubbles. It's the density of the salt water that keeps the bubbles small. If you were to use a protein skimmer in fresh water, the bubbles would be too large and would travel through the water column too quickly to do any good.

UV OR NOT UV?

UV light is a great way to keep parasites under control in the aquarium. However, it does nothing to kill parasites that may be living on the fish themselves because the fish do not pass through the ultraviolet light sterilizer.

Are ultraviolet light sterilizers only for saltwater tanks? Can I use them in freshwater tanks?

Of all the gadgets and technology you can buy, in my opinion, this is the most useful and well worth the money. The very first ultraviolet light sterilizers I encountered in the private sector were used in fish ponds to kill the algae that turn the ponds green. Before you knew it, people were also using them on aquariums.

An ultraviolet bulb is encased in a watertight cylinder. Water is pumped up through the cylinder so that it travels around the bulb, and contact with the bulb kills any parasites or algae in the water. It keeps the water very clear. I have an ultraviolet light sterilizer on every one of my tanks.

If your tank has algae blooms that cause cloudy water, an ultraviolet light sterilizer will literally clear the tank overnight—as long as you use the correct wattage. The bulbs are expensive, and many people will buy sterilizers that don't have sufficient wattage. This is one situation in which more really is better. If you can afford it, always go higher. If the guy in the pet store recommends a 15-watt UV, and you can afford a 25-watt UV, go for it.

I've heard that you shouldn't put an ultraviolet light sterilizer on a brand-new saltwater tank because it will inhibit bacteria growth. Is that true?

I've experimented both with putting the ultraviolet light sterilizer on from the get-go and with waiting until the tank is cycled. I have never noticed any difference. However, the bulbs are expensive and only last for about six months. So if it takes two months to cycle the tank and you only have a couple of groupers in there and parasites are not an issue anyway, then it is more economical to leave the ultraviolet light sterilizer unplugged until the tank is cycled so that you don't waste the bulb.

Sustainability

The problem with collecting saltwater fish is that the sustainability of fish populations is determined by many factors, including multiple government policies and whether they are sustainably managed by those deriving their living directly from them. The quality of saltwater fish collected today is not half as nice as it was ten years ago. This isn't a result of overcollection. The coastal waters of many of the third-world countries where these fish are collected have been polluted by overpopulation and poor agricultural practices. Fish that could previously be collected 5 or 10 miles offshore are now only found much farther out. Bringing the fish back to shore from these greater distances is much more stressful for them.

In a perfect world, we would only purchase saltwater fish bred in captivity. But even though the variety of species bred in captivity is now quite varied, people always want something bigger, flashier, or different. If such fish are available, people will buy them, thus encouraging further collection. My hope is that improved aquaculture techniques will result in more fish being bred in captivity. To me, this is more of a humane, rather than an environmental, issue (though it is the latter as well). It bothers me intensely to see fish collected from their native habitat and shipped halfway around the world only to starve to death in someone's tank. There is no reason for these animals to suffer slow, agonizing deaths. I would be quite happy to sell only aquacultured fish in my store, but if other stores sell collected fish, my customers will go there to buy them. And my rent, taxes, and insurance stay the same either way.

It's not a perfect world, but practices in the marine aquarium trade are ten times better than they were a decade ago, and I am sure they will be even better in the future.

How do you start a saltwater tank?

The first step is to get a second job because everything about a saltwater tank can be more expensive than a freshwater tank. Food, salt, and of course the fish all cost more. However, you can take measures to lessen your expenditures. My first saltwater aquarium was a 10-gallon tank with an undergravel filter run by an air pump, with a layer of dolomite on the bottom. I had two percula clownfish, a camel shrimp, and a scooter blenny. That tank did fine for two years until a hurricane knocked out the electricity and all of my fish died. The clownfish spawned even though there was no anemone. I was quite satisfied with three little fish and a shrimp.

When most people think of a saltwater tank, they imagine lots of expensive reef fish such as butterflies, tangs, and angelfish; live rock; and stony corals. But it can be as simple or involved as you want. There are a hundred ways to set up a 55-gallon saltwater tank. In this chapter I detail the most affordable way.

What is the smallest size saltwater tank that you recommend?

Start with a simple setup. If you don't plan to keep a lot of fish, don't run out to buy the largest tank you can afford—you can do fine with a smaller one. Today, there are also high-tech tanks with built-in filtration and powerful lighting systems for little tiny reefs in tanks as small as 10 gallons. My first saltwater tank was 10 gallons. This size is fine as long as you are content with a scooter blenny, a percula clown, and a blue damsel. That is the maximum number of fish you can expect to keep in a tank this size. However, a freshwater tank with three or four hatchetfish at the surface, a school of tetras in the middle, three or four catfish at the bottom, and maybe a couple pairs of live bearers such as guppies would have looked much better. My 10-gallon saltwater tank with three little fish really looked barren and empty. It was like a little black-and-white TV. A 10-gallon freshwater tank stocked with the right species will look like a giant-screen plasma TV in comparison.

SALTWATER 101

What specific pieces of equipment do I need to set up a saltwater tank?

Get an undergravel filter and two powerheads or strong air pumps to run it. I prefer powerheads because there is less salt splash, but air pumps work fine, too. You need a strong canister filter and eventually an ultraviolet light sterilizer, which is probably the most expensive piece of equipment you will require. If your funds are limited, you can wait a couple of months before adding the UV sterilizer to your setup. Put the undergravel filter in the bottom of the tank and cover it with a 2-inch layer of crushed coral gravel. Years ago, we used dolomite, but crushed coral gravel is much cleaner.

You also need a heater. The older versions hang on the inside of the tank and are a little tricky to control. Now we have totally submersible heaters that can be programmed by simply turning a dial to the desired temperature.

Affix the powerheads to the top of each undergravel filter, place the submersible heater in the bottom of the tank, and conceal it with a piece of decorative coral or a rock. Fill the tank with water, mix salt with very hot water in a bucket, and keep mixing until it is completely dissolved before pouring it in the aquarium. If you pour the salt directly into the tank, it may take weeks to completely dissolve. Then plug in the powerheads and get the undergravel filter going. Along with a layer of floss and some carbon, I like to put a bag of crushed coral in the canister filter for more biological filtration to polish the water. Set that on the tank and get it going. Be sure that the return stem from the filter is just below the surface. You want the surface of the water to be moving without actually breaking. More surface break means more salt splash. Get a tight-fitting glass canopy with a light strip on top. Now your saltwater tank is ready.

What kinds of decorations and equipment should I get for my saltwater tank?

Years ago, we decorated our tanks with dead coral, not realizing the ecological catastrophe produced by breaking up coral reefs and killing the coral for this. These days, beautiful fiberglass decorations are available; these can be easily

Heating the Old Way

Back in the 1960s, a newfangled aquarium heater, which hooked onto the inside of the tank, became available. It basically consisted of two glass tubes connected with a wire: one tube was the thermostat; the other, the heating element. Eventually, someone got the bright idea to incorporate the heating element and the thermostat into one glass tube, but this model also hung on the side of the tank. To set the thermostat, you would turn a little dial at the top of the heater to open or close the coils to engage the heating element and turn it on. When the heating element clicked on, a little orange light on the side of the heater would light up. You turned the knob until the heating element went on, then waited until the water in the tank hit the desired temperature. Once the water was the right temperature, you then had to turn the thermostat down until the little light started flickering on and off. At that point, the thermostat was set to the right temperature. This was very time consuming, but it was the only option. The biggest problem with these heaters was that they would break when water inevitably got into the seal.

removed and cleaned. They are expensive, however, and you don't need to purchase them right away. It's going to take eight weeks to cycle the tank to get it ready for your fish. If your funds are limited, there is no point in getting the ultraviolet light sterilizer or the expensive decorations.

What about water-testing supplies? What will I need?

Next you will need to buy a hydrometer to test the water before you put in the fish. A hydrometer doesn't actually test the salinity; it tests the specific gravity. Saltwater fish can survive in specific gravities ranging from 1.012 to 1.028. (Of course, every time I say this, someone tells me they have fish surviving in a specific gravity higher or lower than this.)

When you fill your 55-gallon tank and add the box of salt for 50 gallons, it usually produces a specific gravity of 1.022 to 1.024. This is fine for fish, but most aquarists will add more fresh water to bring the specific gravity down to 1.018. Saltwater parasites do not thrive in lower specific gravities.

In addition to the hydrometer, you need a test kit. Most of them have reactors to measure pH, ammonia, nitrites, and nitrates. The pH of your water will be perfect at first because of the buffers in the salt mix and the natural buffering ability of the crushed coral. However, these buffers run out quickly, and the pH level of a saltwater tank is in a perpetual state of decline. You must test your pH weekly to ensure that it remains around 8.2. Certain fish, such as triggerfish, will faint if the pH drops. Many times, aquarists call to tell me that all of their fish are fine except for the triggers. When I tell them to test the pH, they discover that it's very low. When it goes up, those fish come right back to life. Pet shops also sell buffering reagents to raise the pH level.

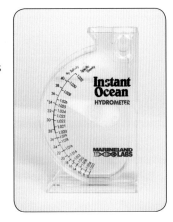

What fish do you recommend for my first saltwater tank?

The first thing you need to buy is some sort of grouper that is about 4 or 5 inches long. This is a very hardy fish that will excrete ammonia and be able to survive in the polluted water for eight weeks while the tank cycles.

Years ago, we used damselfish for this since groupers were very expensive. Half of the damselfish would survive the cycle, but the surviving fish were so fast that it was impossible to get them out of the tank afterward.

Put a couple of flower pots in the tank so that the grouper has a hiding place. Be sure to get a grouper that is well acclimated because it will probably be too frightened to eat for the first couple of days. Before you buy it, ask the pet-store clerk to feed it so that you can be sure it's eating frozen food. Don't buy the grouper unless it's well acclimated to eating frozen food.

After the grouper has been in the tank for about a week, the ammonia level will become extremely high for another two weeks or so. During that time, the grouper will probably have an extreme headache, but it should still eat normally. After that, the ammonia level will drop and the nitrite level will rise for about four weeks. The water may become so toxic that the grouper will stop eating. But if it is a well-acclimated fish, it should survive the cycle. When the nitrite level drops to 0, your tank can be considered cycled. But the nitrite test kit must say 0. Many people will put nitrite reactors in the water, and the nitrite level is very low at first. But the readings will start creeping up after ten minutes, so do not dump the reactors out after a minute or two just because you are anxious to stock the tank with fish. You will know when the level really does get to 0 because the grouper's color and eating habits will return to normal. This is when you can add decorations and your ultraviolet light sterilizer.

How do I deal with the possibilities of parasites in a marine tank?

It is important to use an ultraviolet light sterilizer and maintain a low level of copper in the aquarium. Fish kept in saltwater tanks are mostly wild-caught. Although aquaculture has improved immeasurably, wild-caught fish still far outnumber captive-bred fish. Most of these former fish come loaded with parasites. The ultraviolet light sterilizer should be mounted to the outtake of your canister filter. As the water runs through it, any free-swimming parasites are killed by the ultraviolet light. However, this won't kill parasites living on the fish. This is why it's essential to have a low level of copper when adding wild-caught fish to a tank. Copper solution and a test kit can be found at any pet shop. According to the directions, the copper level in the tank should be 0.15. But the copper is meant to prevent parasites from flourishing and taking over the tank. A level of 0.05 parts per million is just fine. I was forever putting too much copper in my tanks until my good friend Pete Ponciato, the director of the New York Aquarium, taught me how to keep the copper level exactly right. It's a bit tricky. You must add a little copper and measure it, then add a little more and measure again. It takes a while. Until you learn how to do this,

it's better to keep the grouper in the tank than add long-nosed butterflies and other delicate fish.

When your copper level is right, you can start adding fish.

If I use a grouper for cycling the tank, what should I do with it afterward?

The poor grouper really suffered getting your tank cycled, so it seems kind of a shame to get rid of it because you don't want it in your tank. Some groupers will get along with other fish, so you should at least give it a chance. If you are going to keep other groupers, triggerfish, lionfish, eels, grunts, or wrasses, it might mix with them just fine. However, if you plan to keep midwater-feeding fish such as butterflies or cardinal fish, you will have to find another home for the grouper.

The biggest problem when adding new fish to the tank is that the bacteria bed in the undergravel and canister filters will accommodate the waste products of the one fish currently in the tank. If you suddenly add five or six more fish, you will have a spike in ammonia and nitrite until bacteria grows in response to this surge in ammonia. Add the fish one at a time, and wait a week before adding another one.

It's also important to choose fish that are well acclimated and accustomed to captivity. Always ask the pet-shop employees to feed a fish some kind of processed food. This way, you can be sure the fish will eat when you get it home. I have often cautioned people not to buy fish that I just got into my store because they are not eating. But people are confident that the fish will eat once they get it home. What do they have in their tank at home, holy water? If the fish won't eat in the store, why will it eat in a home tank?

How many fish is too many for a tank?

You should also be aware of how many fish a 55-gallon tank (or one of any other size) can accommodate. Fish come in all shapes and sizes. A tank may comfortably hold only one grouper or eel but twenty or thirty very small fish. This depends on the bacteria bed and frequency of water changes. Once you have added all of the fish, you can stop maintaining the copper level. Carbon removes copper. When we set up the tank, we put some carbon in the filter to polish the water. But after eight or more weeks, the copper-removing properties of that carbon have greatly diminished. When you change the floss in the canister filter, you don't need to change the carbon as long as you want to maintain the tank's copper level. It's almost guaranteed that as soon as you decide to stop maintaining the copper level, you will see a new fish that you really want to add to the tank. In this case, buy the fish and ask the pet shop to hold it for a few days while you restore the copper level to your tank.

What are the primary weekly chores I need to perform?

When all is said and done, all you must do on a weekly basis is test the pH, ammonia, and nitrite levels and do a 5-gallon water change. A water change is not the same as adding water that has been lost through evaporation. Some people do monthly water changes of 25 or 30 gallons, but that is so time consuming and makes such a mess. Changing that much water can also stress the fish. It is much easier to keep 5 gallons of pre-mixed salt water handy, siphon any uneaten food and fish waste from the bottom of the tank, and replace that water with the pre-mixed water.

Of course, the procedures I've outlined are very basic. Many other products and methods can be used. But for a 55-gallon tank containing only fish, this method is perfect. I've kept tanks like this going for fifteen years. I kept a powder blue tang in a tank like this for more than ten years. Like my friend Pete told me many years ago, if it ain't broke, don't fix it.

Are clownfish a good choice for a beginner saltwater fish keeper?

Clownfish are absolutely my favorite, favorite, favorite fish. The first saltwater fish I ever owned were two percula clowns, and there's never been a time in my life that I didn't have percula clowns since then. And I love watching *Finding Nemo* over and over again, as do my two little nephews—they act it out together and have every word memorized (although, the first time I showed them a tank full of percula clowns, they looked at them for a minute and then said, "That's not Nemo! These fish can't talk!" What am I supposed to say to that?). The nice thing about clownfish these days is that they are 100 percent aquacultured. Clownfish are bred in facilities all over the world and are now as domesticated as goldfish. Having a tank full of percula clowns, clarkia clownfish, saddle clownfish, or any aquacultured clownfish does not alter the earth's ecological balance in any way. These fish are extremely hardy and forgiving. They eat prepared foods. They can tolerate many changes in water chemistry that would kill fish such as butterflies and angels.

A tank full of clownfish always looks impressive and will attract the admiration of your family members and guests.

What are the potential pitfalls for saltwater aquarists who tend to purchase their marine organisms on impulse?

The problem that many people encounter when purchasing both saltwater and freshwater organisms is not being aware of water chemistry when purchasing them. It's important that the water chemistry of your tank is the same as that to which the animal you're purchasing is accustomed. A piece of coral that is completely extended and flourishing in the pet shop will do equally well in your home tank if the water quality and chemistry is exactly the same. If you want to bring this animal home, put a deposit on it and take home a sample of water so you can test it and adjust the water in your tank accordingly. This avoids subjecting the animal to any stress with water when it goes into your aquarium. It is also important to ask questions before purchasing any animal. Many times, people want to buy fish in my store, but I tell them to wait because the fish isn't eating yet. If the fish is not eating despite my constant fussing, a change is not likely to improve matters. More likely, the fish will die.

What are some of the hardiest and easy-to-care for marine fish for beginning marine aquarists?

As a rule, if you can duplicate the animal's diet and environment, it will do well in captivity. All saltwater fish need the same basic water chemistry, but they vary in feeding and living habits. Saltwater fish that are *pelagic*—in other words, never in the same place twice, and are harder to care for than sedentary fish such as groupers, clownfish, eels, and hawkfish, which can be comfortable in a small amount of space. Opportunistic eating habits also make a fish adaptable to captivity. The fish I just mentioned will accept quite a few different foods. They are always easier to keep than specialized feeders such as butterfly fish and angelfish. Of course, even some species within the butterfly fish genus will thrive in captivity better than others. The only way to determine this on an individual level is to ask questions before buying the fish.

My Early Years as a Fish Keeper

As kids, most our time was centered on our 10-gallon aquariums. We had no Internet. And there were no after-school sports for me and my friends because we were all nerds. Television was limited to three network channels, two local channels, and one PBS channel.

The only way we could learn about fish was by reading the books that were available, particularly those by Dr. Innes, and my favorite magazine, *Tropical Fish Hobbyist.* When it arrived in the mail, I grabbed it, ran into my room, and read it from cover to cover. In the 1970s, PBS aired a series called *Guppies to Groupers,* hosted by Paul Speice. Every week, he gave a lesson in fish keeping on subjects ranging from salt-water fish to live-bearing fish. It was filmed in a studio with a 200-gallon tank in the middle and smaller tanks along the back walls. Every week, they were set up differently with different types of fish. This must have been an extremely expensive show to produce on a small public-television budget.

The information that Paul offered on that show was timeless; it is as valid to-day as it was then. Paul is one of my heroes, and today he writes a very good monthly column for the magazine *Freshwater and Marine Aquarium*. Who would have suspected that I would have my fish on TV thirty years after first watching Paul's show? I can now appreciate the amount of work that went into each one of his segments.

Decades ago, our home aquariums were made from stainless steel frames with slate bottoms, and the glass was affixed to the frames with heavy black tar. They all had little vibrating air pumps and clear plastic box filters filled with charcoal and glass wool, which our fathers had to cut for us because we always got our hands full of glass splinters when we tried to do it. All the kids had aquariums like this. But every neighborhood also had a real fish keeper who had big tanks and a big supreme Aquamaster air pump with a piston belt. This person was always treated with great respect by the rest of us.

As kids, our favorite pastime was to breed live-bearing fish and trade them with one another. We bred platys, swordtails, guppies, and mollies. I loved crossing different-colored fish to see what color offspring they would produce.

Money was always tight, but fortunately most fish were pretty cheap back then. That is, until the very first fancy guppies came on the market. Before then, the guppies kept as aquarium fish were the ones now used as feeder fish. The fish that are sold in pet shops as feeder guppies today were the pet guppies of choice back in the 1960s. They were very colorful but quite small. Spontaneous mutations, such as larger size, larger fins, and more distinct colors, occurred among those guppies. Breeders capitalized on those mutations to produce different breeds of guppies. The first fancy-tailed guppies appeared in pet stores in the 1960s, and we found them fascinating. The only obstacle was the price. They were $10 a pair, which was quite expensive then. After much debate, my friends and I pooled our financial resources and went to the pet store with $5. We bought the most pregnant-looking fancy guppy and flipped baseball cards to determine who got to keep that fish in a breeding trap in his home aquarium. When it had babies, we divided them up.

After the new fancy guppy breeds became firmly established, the original wild form of guppy fell from favor. Now, fifty years later, those fish are unfortunately sold as feeder fish.

Will different species of tetras school together? It would make sense with neons and cardinals, as they are of similar size and color, but what about serpae tetras, which are a different color and slightly larger than neons and cardinals?

Serpae tetras, by the way, are one of my favorite tetras, and I will never forget the day I bought my first one. Given a choice, I would prefer not to school the different tetras together. If you have four cardinal tetras and one serpae tetra, most likely they will stay apart. However, if a threatening situation arises, blood is no longer thicker than water in the minds of the fish, and different species will school together to confuse a common enemy. This could be prompted by sudden movement outside the tank or a net thrust into the water.

However, different shapes and sizes characterize different fish species, and in an ideal situation, different species will not school together. But this is not an ideal world, and every fish is an individual. Just as terrestrial animals form associations, different fish can also do this even if it is not to their evolutionary advantage.

Can barbs and tetras be mixed?

When I was about seven, I bought a tiger barb for my 10-gallon community tank. Back then, we collected cans and saved up money to buy fish, so we always bought them one at a time. I vividly remember watching this tiger barb rush up to my other fish and nip their fins. Every time the fish did that, I tapped

the glass, hoping to discourage it through negative reinforcement, the same way I trained my dog. It never worked because negative reinforcement must be done every single time the behavior happens. Judging by the condition of the fins on my other fish, this happened all day long while I was at school. The half hour I spent each day trying to train this tiger barb would not have made a difference.

I went back to the pet store and talked to the man who sold me this fish, Al Selmer, who still owns Selmer's Pet Land in Huntington, Long Island, New York. He told me that tiger barbs are schooling fish. In a school, they behave like a big loud family, always arguing. Al suggested that I get two or three more tiger barbs; they would stay together, argue among themselves, and leave the other fish alone. Fortunately, my dad gave me an advance on my allowance, and I was able to buy two more tiger barbs to keep company with my fin-nipper. Al was right. They stayed together and annoyed each other all day long and left my other fish alone.

So yes, barbs and tetras can get along if you keep the tiger barbs in groups so they can gossip together rather than bothering the tetras.

How are colors and finnages created in guppies?

The natural color patterns of guppies are highly variable. They are encoded in the guppies' DNA and manifest through random mutations. It's up to the fish breeder to spot these spontaneous mutations in color or fin shape and preserve these traits through selective breeding. This is done by breeding the mutated fish back to one of its parents or a sibling to perpetuate the mutation. The colors are induced by nature. Nowadays, fish colors can be manipulated through genetic engineering: one example is the Glo-Fish, which is a type of zebra danio.

Has there ever been a planted goldfish tank that was successful?

Goldfish do like to eat many aquatic plants, but not all of them. They also can be beneficial to some plants, such as broadleaf sword plants and Java ferns. Goldfish don't find these plants palatable at all and usually prefer not to eat them, but they still try, and as they chew on the plants, they do a fine job of controlling hair algae. As a rule, these plants do fine in goldfish tanks. Of course, if you plant your goldfish tank with elodea or cabomba, you will be inviting trouble.

Why are freshwater fish typically less flashy than (not as colorful as) saltwater fish?

As a general rule, an animal is brightly colored to make it more readily recognized by other members of its species from a distance. Birds, butterflies, and marine fish travel vast distances. Their bright colors and patterns make it easier for them to recognize one another from far away.

Should salt ever be added to a freshwater aquarium? What would be a situation in which you might use salt?

Years ago, we never used salt in aquariums except to treat freshwater fish for ich. Just as a freshwater bath will kill the ich on a saltwater fish, putting a freshwater fish with freshwater ich into salt water will change the osmotic pressure and kill the ich.

We never really put salt in the tanks for the fish to live in. The fish were always kept in pure fresh water, and we always had lots of live plants in the aquariums, which the salt would have damaged. However, in this day and age, many of the fish we commonly keep, such as fancy goldfish and many tetras, are bred in Pacific Rim countries where the water naturally has lots of salt. These fish are technically bred in almost brackish water. When they are imported from the Far East, they must have salt in the water to thrive. They are acclimated to water with a specific gravity different from what comes out of your tap.

Of course, this doesn't apply to all fish. If you are keeping fish from Florida or South America, additional salt is not necessary. But if you are keeping fish imported from the Far East, find out whether they were exported from an area with naturally salty water. This is the only way to estimate the amount of salt to put in your home aquarium to keep those fish happy. In general, fish can accommodate slight changes in osmotic pressure.

What type of water do mollies prefer (brackish, salt water, fresh water)? Does their hybridization change what type of water they need now, versus their natural habitat?

Like many freshwater fish, mollies are fairly adaptable. In the past, we always kept them in salt water, and they were commonly used to cycle saltwater tanks. Their natural habitat is brackish, high-alkaline water. Most of the mollies sold in pet shops these days are bred in the Far East, where the water has extremely high concentrations of salt. Unfortunately, when they are purchased here, they are usually placed into freshwater tanks with very little salt, which is fatal for them. However, Florida-raised mollies can still be found in some smaller pet shops. These will do fine in a freshwater tank as long as the pH is monitored and the fish receive the proper diet.

I have a 55-gallon tank at home that is heavily planted with lots of algae, where I raise my own strain of black mollies. I've raised the same strain of fish in this tank for more than eight years, and there isn't one drop of salt in the water. These fish are gorgeous. The males are more than 2 inches long. They are jet black and, oddly enough, over the generations they have developed orange borders on their dorsal and tail fins. When the tank becomes overpopulated, I take some out and bring them to my pet store, where they are sold instantly. The people who buy them have success with them because they are acclimated to totally fresh water.

What are the most important aspects of keeping mollies?

Every spring, I put sailfin mollies in my backyard fish ponds, which contain no salt water. The fish do absolutely fabulous, and by fall these ponds are brimming with sailfin mollies of every color, shape, and size. So salt level is just one aspect of husbandry. Diet is equally important. The mollies in these ponds have an extremely varied diet of mosquito larvae and lots of algae. These ponds are specially designed. Although there is one deep area, most of the water is only about 6 inches deep. The mollies, guppies, and swordtails spend most of their time in these shallow areas with lots of aquatic plants.

Unfortunately, not many pet-store owners are as into their fish as I am, so it's hard to find mollies that are acclimated to pure fresh water. The closest thing you can find are mollies bred on good old-fashioned farms in Florida. When I was a kid, all of our live-bearing fish came from farms such as these. We had no trouble keeping the fish alive, which is not always the case with live-bearing fish imported from the Far East. When buying mollies in a pet store, always ask where they came from so that you can duplicate this water quality in your home aquarium.

What would happen if a red guppy mated with a white guppy?

As a general rule, red is dominant to white. If the strains were pure, and you then mated two of those red babies, 25 percent of the resulting offspring would be red visually and genetically, 50 percent would be red visually but carry the white gene, and 25 percent would be white. However, unless your guppies came from a breeder who raises pure strains, it is impossible to know the genetic heritage of the parents, and the resulting babies could be any color.

Can closely related fish in the same genus interbreed? Why can Endler's and regular guppies do that?

Most animals that can be hybridized must belong to the same genus, but there are exceptions. Sometimes hybrids produced by two animals from the same genus produce fertile offspring, but not always. Endler's guppies are closely related to the guppies traditionally kept in fish tanks. They belong to the same genus of brackish-water fish *Poecilia* in the family Poeciliidae of the order Cyprinodontiformes. They were named by Dr. John Endler in 1975. They prefer hard, warm water like regular guppies do. They can be crossed with regular guppies to produce fertile offspring. However, this is not considered good husbandry because Endler's guppies are uncommon, and hybridization dilutes their gene pool.

There is currently some discussion that the Endler's guppy is really not a guppy but a different species. Even though it may not be in the same genus as the guppy, it is possible for two fish to interbreed that are not in the same genus. Other live-bearing fish that can be interbred include guppies and mollies, and platys and swordtails. The mollie-guppy crosses are not fertile, but the platy-swordtail crosses are.

The Downfall of the King

When I was a kid, the king of the freshwater fish hobby was the freshwater angelfish. Every novice aquarist could choose from among the hundreds of baby angelfish found in every pet store. A pet store might have ten tanks full of different types of angelfish, such as black, marbled, and silver angelfish. We bought them as tiny babies, about the size of your pinkie nail. Over the next six months, we would watch them grow into their full magnificence.

Then, about thirty years ago, a virus attacked all freshwater angelfish populations. Commercial production of them in the United States ground to a halt. The only ones available came from a few private breeders or the Far East. This virus is so insidious that when a new strain of angelfish comes in contact with it, the fish die within a week. Even angelfish purchased from private breeders (and thus with no exposure to the virus) will succumb to the virus when they get to a pet store. Because so many fish come from the Far East, most pet stores always seem to harbor this virus. It is still not under control. Most pet stores no longer carry freshwater angelfish for this reason. I find this such a pity, because keeping angelfish was such an enjoyable part of my childhood.

Why do bettas fight?

Most male animals will fight over territory. Anyone who has fished in a freshwater lake in early summer has probably seen nests of sunfish evenly spaced apart in shallow water. As soon as one male leaves his nest and ventures into another's territory, they will fight in the same way that bettas do. This is true of most fish that build nests or keep their fry confined to one area, as most South American cichlids do. Even saltwater clownfish will fight any other male clownfish that comes near their nests. Bettas have such a reputation as fighters because as labyrinth fish they can extract oxygen from air and live in small enclosed spaces. They are easily kept in captivity. Human nature being what it is, people have enjoyed watching bettas fight, and this has evolved into an organized activity complete with betting. This is very popular in Southeast Asia. Bettas are not the only creatures subjected to this pastime: roosters, crickets, thrushes, donkeys, and rams are used for fighting. But it's a little difficult to stage donkey- and ram-fighting contests in the middle of a big city. That's why fighting bettas became so popular.

My Most Unusual Aquatic Pet

My most unusual aquatic pet wasn't actually a fish, it was a cephalopod. To be specific, it was an Atlantic octopus. One day when I was about fifteen, I went to my favorite aquarium store and for the first time in my life saw a live octopus. And I just had to have it. It cost an incredible amount of money, and the clerk at the pet store had a very difficult time wrestling it into the bag, which fascinated me all the more.

Keep in mind that this was back in the pre-Internet, pre-cable TV days. We only got a glimpse of the natural aquatic world by watching specials produced by the National Geographic Society and Jacques Cousteau. Cousteau once did a special on cephalopods that completely fascinated me. The special demonstrated the intelligence of octopuses by showing how they could open jars to get food. When I saw that octopus in the pet store, that is exactly what I wanted to try to have it do when I got it home.

I took my new octopus home and put it in my 55-gallon saltwater aquarium. The aquarium was set up with an undergravel filter, a layer of dolomite (a type of crushed coral) on top, and an old Supreme Powermaster mechanical filter hanging on the back. That was the extent of saltwater technology in those days, but the fish did just fine. The next day, I checked on my new octopus and promptly discovered that it had eaten all of the fish in the tank with the exception of one lionfish and one domino damsel. I had known that octopuses ate crustaceans, but I had no idea that they also ate fish. However, the octopus continued to share the tank with those two remaining fish for the next year.

In that time, I managed to teach Otto the octopus to open jars to get shrimp out of them. The staple of his diet was cocktail shrimp from the local grocery store, supplemented with some feeder goldfish and killies that I caught in a nearby canal. Otto became quite friendly. When I put my hand into the tank, he would swim over and grasp my hand with his tentacles. I never quite knew whether Otto was prompted to show affection for me or he just wanted to eat me. He would actually open the tank cover and stick his tentacles out to grab my hand and pull it in. Once, to my surprise, the octopus climbed out of the aquarium, and I found him scuttling across the floor. I quickly put him back and kept the cover taped down from then on.

Otto had incredible dexterity. He was always rearranging the rocks and corals in the tank to create new hiding places for himself, much to the dismay, I'm sure, of the domino damsel, which also liked hiding in those rocks. I enjoyed Otto's company for an entire year. Unfortunately, one day he pulled the heater into the tank and took it apart, electrocuting himself, the domino damsel, and the lionfish, and blowing all of the circuits in that part of the house.

I have owned and sold hundreds of octopuses since then. Frankly, I don't know if it was because I had more time back then, or Otto really was smarter than most of his kind, but I have never seen one to match his personality and intelligence.

I saw an ad online for dwarf seahorses. I'm willing to make another 20-gallon aquarium for them when I find more research on this fish. Has anyone kept them successfully?

This brings back memories of my youth. In those days, every comic book contained ads for dwarf Atlantic seahorses. For only $5.99, you got a pregnant male and two females; the ad claimed that "the pregnant male could have up to twenty-two babies, giving you a total of twenty-five seahorses." So you collected enough cans to earn the money and mailed it to Florida.

About six weeks later, you got a little bag in the mail containing the seahorses swimming in aimless circles with their tails hooked together, a package of sea salt, and a package of brine shrimp eggs. You would take a goldfish bowl, add the sea salt, and put the seahorses in. Next, you would hatch the brine shrimp eggs. As they hatched, you would siphon them off with an eyedropper and put them in the bowl for the seahorses to eat. Amazingly enough, these little seahorses sometimes survived this way for two or three weeks. This shows you how hardy they can be.

If kept in a 20-gallon aquarium, with a gentle biological filter, some live rock, and a power compact light, these dwarf seahorses do quite well. Every time I see them, I think of those comic books of my childhood. In addition to seahorses, you could also order squirrel monkeys and baby raccoons from the backs of these comic books!

What do sea urchins eat, and how can you replicate this in a saltwater aquarium?

In nature, most sea urchins graze on rocks, and it is very hard to replicate this in an aquarium. The live rocks we keep in aquariums can only grow so many organisms. I have seen sea urchins crawling over bits of fish food on the bottoms of tanks. The food disappears as the sea urchin passes over, so

MARC MORRONE

Kids and Fish

Many years ago when I started keeping fish, the hobby attracted an equal number of adults and children of every age. They all seemed to have the same interests in fish, the same concerns for their welfare and husbandry, and mostly a great deal of curiosity about different species. Today, it seems that most of the aquarists coming into my store are adults. It's rare that a child will come in and ask me questions about different fish. Children do come in with their parents to buy pets. I ask them what kind of fish they have at home, and they usually shrug their shoulders and tell me that some are red, some are silver, and some are black.

I understand that the world is a different place today. Kids can't jump on their bicycles with a pocket full of change and ride off to the local pet store. Even so, I can't understand why kids who have home aquariums don't show more interest. They basically leave it to their parents, and their involvement is limited to occasionally looking at the fish. I can only blame this on the virtual world.

I am mystified that a child can learn every detail about a particular Pokemon animal—its likes and dislikes, natural habitat, and history. Yet, they have no interest in learning about a guppy or mollie living in a tank in their house. It's a pity that so many schools don't have fish clubs or natural history clubs for children who might have a passion for this. All of the kids I knew who played a musical instrument in school, including myself, have not continued as adults, yet many who kept fish as kids still maintain this hobby. I suppose the problem is that so few teachers have the interest, time, or resources to introduce children to fish keeping.

We sell lots of fish at my store, and fish keeping will always be here, but I guess the days are gone when wide-eyed kids would come in with a ruler to measure fish and calculate if they can fit one more into their home aquarium. The rule was 1 inch of fish per gallon of water, and we were always fudging the numbers to try and squeeze one more in. It's been many years since I have seen a kid express that kind of interest in fish keeping.

If you have kids in your life—your children, nieces, nephews, grandchildren, students—why not try to introduce them to the many joys of aquariums and the fascinating fish that inhabit them? You could open a whole new world of wonders to them.

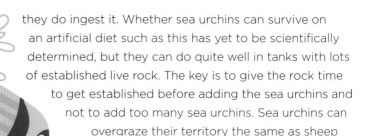

they do ingest it. Whether sea urchins can survive on an artificial diet such as this has yet to be scientifically determined, but they can do quite well in tanks with lots of established live rock. The key is to give the rock time to get established before adding the sea urchins and not to add too many sea urchins. Sea urchins can overgraze their territory the same as sheep and cattle can.

How long is the life span of anemones? What can you feed them to keep them healthy and happy?

Most anemones in captivity don't live long at all because they are not properly cared for. However, my cousin Brian has had an anemone in his reef tank for six years, and it regularly reproduces via division. Most anemones will eat any saltwater protein-type food, such as clams, silversides, and shrimp. But this is only part of their diet. Their bulk of their color derives from symbiotic algae that live within them. These algae will die if the anemone is not kept in the proper lighting. Once the symbiotic algae die, the anemone is doomed because it is unable to properly digest food without its host algae. The little aiptasia (triffid, glass, rock) anemones that are such pests in some marine aquariums are an ugly brown color because they do not have symbiotic algae living inside them. They can therefore survive on almost any protein source. The big colorful ones need much more care.

What type of fish are African dwarf frogs compatible with? What food do they eat? Do they need a "land" area, or are they fine just swimming around?

These frogs, also called Xenopus, are among my favorite aquatic creatures. However, they usually don't mix well with fish. If you get a very small one and allow it to grow up in a tank with fish, it usually won't bother the fish. All

of the animals will be acclimated to one another. However, if you buy a full-grown frog and add it to a tank containing fish that are small enough to fit in the frog's mouth, it will usually eat them—or at least try to, which will certainly stress the fish. When I raised African frogs as a kid, I fed them earthworms, crickets, and goldfish. These frogs grew up to be voracious hunters. To them, anything that moved was a possible food source.

If you get a very small African frog and raise it on pelleted foods, there is a good chance it will not consider fish as a food source. Then again, I could be wrong and it may grow up and decide to eat all of your fish. So this may require a bit of experimentation. Most fish-food flakes don't fit easily into the frogs' mouths. They need a food that is round or oval, and they use their little front feet to stuff it into their mouths.

These frogs are totally aquatic and will not come out of the water at all. If you do put one on land, it slithers along in a rather pathetic way. The African frog is unable to hop, crawl, or walk like terrestrial frogs do. But it does make a very engaging pet. It can learn to recognize different people and will come up to the edge of the tank to be fed when it sees you enter the room.

What are the water additive needs for soft corals? Do I need iodine, calcium, strontium, and molybdenum?

Ideally, these invertebrates need all of these plus calcium kalkwasser. Of course, every time I say this, someone sends me a photo of soft coral they raised without any trace minerals or other supplements literally growing out of a reef tank. Still, aquatic chemists have documented the needs of sessile invertebrates, and those needs are very real, though they may vary slightly in different aquarium environments. Before you try to grow hard or soft coral, you should know precisely what water chemistry they will need. If you buy them from a pet store or breeder on the Internet or swap cuttings of corals with other members of an aquarium club, ask the seller who has propagated them. This way, you can duplicate the water chemistry in your home aquarium. As I have said before, different aquatic animals can adapt to different water qualities.

Can live rock be used in brackish water?

Live rock contains lots of invertebrate animals. Some saltwater fish can do very well in low salinities. For instance, I have seen some lionfish and groupers kept in salinities as low as 1.012; invertebrates do not thrive in low salinities. Having no skeleton, they are more susceptible to changes in osmotic pressure. If you purchased live rock that was in marine water with a salinity of 1.024 and placed it in brackish water with a salinity level of 1.010, the creatures that make the rock live will die. That's why a freshwater bath works so well for fish suffering from the ich parasite. Because the ich parasites are invertebrates, the fish are better able to withstand the sudden changes in osmotic pressure. It will not harm the fish, but it will kill the parasites. The same thing happens if rock covered with tube worms and small crustaceans is subjected to a sudden change in salinity, which also causes the change in osmotic pressure. More salt in the water makes it denser. This change in density will affect the animals living in that water.

My children caught some tadpoles and water beetles in a nearby pond. Can I add these to my aquarium?

This is never a good idea. As a general rule, wild and domestic animals don't mix very well. Wild animals, such as dragonfly larvae and certain water beetles, can harm your domestic animals. Many of the pond pets, such as tadpoles, die. Tadpoles are actually quite delicate and can be easily injured when captured. Aside from the North American bullfrog, native frog populations are in decline. The less we interfere with them, the better. If you do want to make a temporary habitat for your pond pets, set up an aquarium with its own filter. This way, you can keep them for the summer and release them back into the pond in the fall.